Everyday
Cooking for One

Everyday
Cooking for One

Imaginative, delicious and healthy recipes that make it fun to cook for one

Wendy Hobson

A How To Book

ROBINSON

For Chris and Melissa

ROBINSON

First published in Great Britain in 2012 by Spring Hill
an imprint of How To Books Ltd

This edition published in 2015 by Robinson

A CIP catalogue record for this book is available from the British Library.

ISBN: 978-1-90586-294-8 (paperback)

Produced for How To Books by Deer Park Productions, Tavistock, Devon
Designed and typeset by Mousemat Design Ltd
Printed and bound in Great Britain by Bell & Bain Ltd, Glasgow

Papers used by Robinson are from well-managed forests
and other responsible sources

Robinson
An imprint of
Little, Brown Book Group
Carmelite House
50 Victoria Embankment
London EC4Y 0DZ

An Hachette UK Company
www.hachette.co.uk

www.littlebrown.co.uk

NOTE: The material contained in this book is set out in good faith for general guidance and no liability can be accepted for loss or expense incurred as a result of relying in particular circumstances on statements made in the book. Laws and regulations are complex and liable to change, and readers should check the current position with relevant authorities before making personal arrangements.

How To Books are published by Robinson, an imprint of Little, Brown Book Group. We welcome proposals from authors who have first-hand experience of their subjects. Please set out the aims of your book, its target market and its suggested contents in an email to howto@littlebrown.co.uk

Contents

Cooking for One 9

1 Tasty, Healthy Food for One 11

2 Setting Up Your Kitchen 15

3 The Singles' Storecupboard 18

4 Tips for Beginners 20

5 Soups and Snacks 25

Curried Apple Soup 26

Chicken and Sweetcorn Chowder 27

Butter Bean and Bacon Soup 28

Carrot and Coriander Soup 30

Chilled Almond Soup 31

Traditional Vegetable Soup 32

Beetroot and Brie Toasts 34

Spinach and Avocado Salad with Pancetta 36

Asparagus with Poached Eggs and Parmesan 37

Caramelised Onion and Goats' Cheese Puffs 38

Quick Oriental Prawn Noodles 39

Stilton Pâté 40

Garlic and Caramelised Pepper Bruschetta 41

Ideas for Light Meals 42

6 Seafood 45

Cooking and Serving Fish 46

Crab Balls with Dipping Sauces 47

Prawns in Lime and Chilli Marinade 48

Pan-fried Scallops with Prawns 49

Paprika Seafood and Artichokes 50

Seafood Chive Pancakes 51

Grilled Mackerel with Harissa Couscous 52

Poached Fish with Sweet Potato 53

Salmon with Herb and Garlic Mayonnaise 54

Thai-style Salmon 55

Salmon Fish Balls with Chunky Sauté Chips 56

Sea Bream with Minted Salsa Verde 57

Griddled Sole with Lemon Butter Sauce 58

Niçoise Salad 59

Hake with Pancetta Potatoes 60

Smoked Mackerel Risotto 61

Arancini 62

Smoked Mackerel and Potato Salad 63

7 Beef 65

Home-made Burger with Caramelised Onion
  Chutney 66

Spaghetti and Meatballs with Tomato Sauce 67

Tagliatelle Bolognese 68

Baked Stuffed Mushrooms 70

Beef, Bacon and Egg 71

Beef in Red Wine 72

Minced Beef with Chilli and Kidney Beans 74

Steak with Gorgonzola Mash 75

8 Lamb 77

Lamb with Minted Mash 78

Stuffed Minted Aubergine 80

Lamb Cutlets with Sweet Spinach 81

Lamb Chops with Shallots and Peas 82

Lamb Shank with Rosemary and Garlic 83

Braised Tender Lamb 84

Lamb Steaks with Mustard and Redcurrant 85

9 Pork 87

Pork with Lemon Pasta 88

Pork Rolls with Gorgonzola 89

Pork Tortilla Wrap 90

Pork Escalope with Rhubarb 91

Roast Pork with Gravy 92

Soy Pork Noodles 94

Minced Pork Meatloaf 95

Farm Sausages with Roasted Vegetables 96

Apple Sausages in Redcurrant Gravy 97

Crumble-topped Pork Mince 98

Pork with Grapefruit Sauce 99

10 Chicken and Poultry 101

Chicken and Avocado Salad 102

Chicken with Chorizo and Beans 103

Chicken Thighs with Spicy Dressing 104

Chicken with Raisins and Pine Nuts 105

Roast Lemon-infused Chicken 106

Chicken in Lemon and Tarragon Sauce 108

Chicken with Orange Salad 109

Barbecue-grilled Chicken 110

Coconut Chicken with Sticky Rice 111

Chicken Parcel 112

Crispy Spiced Chicken 113

Minted Chicken Salad 114

Chicken with Stilton Sauce 115

Chicken Korma with Pilau Rice 116

Turkey in Citrus Sauce 117

Turkey Goujons with mushrooms 118

Sweet-glazed Duck 119

11 Vegetables and Pulses 121

Artichokes and Courgettes with Balsamic
    Dressing 122

Aubergine Boats 123

Crunchy Aubergine with Avocado Dip 124

Coleslaw with Apple and Raisins 125

Chickpea and Aubergine Salad with Feta 126

Leek and Gorgonzola Squares 127

Caramelised Red Onion Tart with Carrot
    Salad 128

Ideas for Pasta 129

Potato Pancakes 130

Roast Potatoes with Chorizo 131

Pesto Rice Salad 132

Sweetcorn Pancakes 133

Sweet and Sour Shallots 134

Creamed Sweet Potato with Honey 135

Tomato Sauce 136

Stir-fry Vegetables with Chestnuts 137

Ideas for Salads 138

Salad Dressings 139

12 Eggs and Cheese 141

Pancakes 142

Potato and Onion Frittata 143

Baked Eggs 144

Leek and Gruyère Flan 145

Cranberry and Brie Puffs 146

Piperade 147

Omelette with Lots of Fillings 148

Savoury Egg Rice 149

13 Desserts 151

Chocolate Bread and Butter Pudding 152

Caramelised Pears with Mascarpone 153

Date Pudding with Toffee Sauce 154

Chocolate Pudding with Built-in Sauce 155

Baked Apple with Caramel Sauce 156

Rhubarb Oat Crumble 157

Maple Syrup Tarts 158

Tiny Tiramisu 159

Chocolate Mousse 160

Caramel Oranges 161

Mango Sorbet 162

Grapefruit and Blueberry Brûlée 163

Lemon Curd Ice Cream with Blueberries 164

Microwave Meringues 165

14 Cakes, Biscuits and Treats 167

Cream Tea for One 168

Moist Chocolate Cake with Fresh Cream 169

Lemon Drizzle Cake 170

Toffee and Cherry Squares 171

Honey-drenched Tunisian Almond Cake 172

Old-fashioned Gingerbread 173

Old English Beetroot Cake 174

Chocolate and Nut Fudge Brownies 176

Coconut and Nut Squares 177

Banana and Date Bread 178

Hazelnut Cake with Mocha Filling 179

Mocha and White Choc Chip Cookies 180

Crumbly Honey and Oat Bites 181

Pineapple Upside-down Cake 182

Indulgent Chocolate Fudge 183

15 Meal Planners 185

Index 188

Cooking for One

If you are one of the many people cooking just for yourself, you'll know all about the pros and cons. On the plus side, you can have what you want when you want it, and you can sit down and relax with a glass of wine and a tasty meal – a scenario that many people in busy households can only dream about.

But there are quite a few downsides to balance that scenario:

- Choosing recipes can be tiresome because most recipe books are written for four people. What do you do with that half a tin of tomatoes, and how *do* you quarter an egg?

- Especially when you come in from a long day at work, often you just can't be bothered to make the effort when it's just for you.

- If you do go to the effort, making complicated recipes just for one can feel like a waste of time and energy.

- Smaller sizes cost more, and buy-one-get-one-free offers take up cupboard space for months.

It's too easy to be put off by what should be a great opportunity because, after all, you have only yourself to please! So this book is about turning what could be a chore into a highlight.

Let's assume you enjoy sitting down to a tasty meal at the end of the day to relax and just for its own sake. You like to experiment with new things but you have your own old favourites that perhaps could do with refreshing. Time is critical; healthy is important; and your watchwords are 'simple but delicious'.

These recipes offer you the chance to fulfil all those criteria, and to overcome the major hassles we identified too, by showing you how to create a storecupboard of ingredients to act as a backdrop for your cooking.

There are recipes designed just for one, using convenient ingredients – chicken pieces, single vegetables, small packs or tins – and not just quartered versions of family meals. Plus, if you can't avoid a leftover item, there will be a partner recipe to use it up, or a simple suggestion so nothing goes to waste.

Then there are those dishes that really need to be cooked in larger quantities because you cannot make them just for one: cakes, casseroles and the like. But if you make these when you fancy doing a bit of cooking, then divide up the spoils into individual portions for freezing – you can serve these remaining portions in different ways to create new dishes. Plus, all through the book, there are quick ideas, hints and tips.

So this book is really about bringing the fun back into everyday cooking for one. It doesn't use obscure ingredients, it uses short-cuts when it wants to, it blends flavours from one continent with ingredients from another without the slightest worry about authenticity, and all it aims to do is to help you put a delicious and nutritious meal on your plate at the end of a busy day.

And because some people cooking for themselves are new to it, I've included plenty of information to help you find your way round a recipe and gain the confidence to really enjoy yourself in the kitchen.

So, set the table, pour yourself a glass of some frivolous little number you picked up on special offer (aren't screw-caps brilliant?), sit down to your simply prepared but quite delicious supper, relax and enjoy.

Tasty, Healthy Food for One

CHAPTER

1

Eating a healthy, balanced and enjoyable diet is not rocket science. It's a case of:

- Plenty of fresh fruit and veg

- A moderate portion of unrefined carbohydrates

- A little fat … and a little of what you fancy

If we believed the media every time they home in on one ingredient or another, we'd get a constantly changing picture because they tend to shed a blinding light on just one thing, throwing everything else into shadow. Take butter, for example. One minute it is a silent killer – loading your arteries with saturated animal fats. The next minute, it is the most natural food in the world. The fact is that neither extreme is true. Butter is a natural food, free of additives and free of the results of over-processing. It is also a saturated fat, which means we should not include too much in our diet. It's a case of a little of what you fancy.

Consult a nutritionist and they would be able to break down this simplistic view and give you the full, complex picture of our dietary needs. But at its most basic, your plate should be half vegetables or fruit, just over a quarter protein foods, such as meat or fish, and the rest made up of foods containing fats and natural sugars.

When you are cooking for yourself, it can be more difficult to maintain these principles because you have to maintain your own motivation – there's no one to compliment, support or criticise. The best way to counter that is to work on a routine that makes planning, cooking and eating an enjoyable part of your day. Get yourself into generally good habits – they are much harder to break than principles – but always be flexible. Let common sense rule.

Making it easy

The recipes here employ a convenient strategy based on a kind of divide-and-conquer principle, with the secret weapon being the freezer.

- **Select for convenience:** Buy steaks, chops, fish fillets and all the things that are easy to divide up and cook for one.

- **Shop and freeze:** Don't just put items in the freezer in packs as you buy them; divide them into individual portions before you freeze them.

- **Prepare and freeze:** Prepare some things before you freeze them, such as meatballs.

- **Cook and freeze:** Cook in larger quantities, then freeze separate portions to eat another time.

- **Cook complementary recipes:** If you use half a tin or packet of something in one recipe, make something else to use up the remainder.

- **Save energy:** If you are cooking something in the oven, then choose something else to cook with it so you don't waste the energy.

- **Defrost and reinvent:** Recreate new flavours with the dishes you have frozen.

What's in the cupboard?

Your first good habit begins with setting up your storecupboard, following the ideas offered in Chapter 3. If you have a cupboard of basics at the ready – a few tins, jars and packets – it makes it so much easier to make interesting dishes – especially of the last-minute variety.

Don't rush out and buy everything on the list as there are bound to be items that you will end up not using. Start with a few obvious items – oil, butter, salt and pepper, stock – then gradually add more things as you work through the recipes until you build up something that suits your style and taste. Your storecupboard items will provide the foundations for the fresh foods you buy as and when it suits.

Solving the issue of quantities

Generally you can buy fresh vegetables in whatever quantity you need, the notable exceptions being celery and cabbage. Since I like to use a stick of celery in the base of many dishes, I've included a celery soup on page 32, salad ideas on page 138.

Another thing you can do is think about the actual ingredients you buy. Buy shallots instead of onions, Brussels instead of cabbage, individual fruit in preference to bags, chicken breasts, salmon steaks, fish fillets, lamb chops or pork cutlets – all ideal for cooking for one.

Cans, however, can be more problematic as most are around 400g, which is usually more than you need for one portion. But we'll cook in four-person quantities, then divide and freeze; we'll pair recipes so you can use half in each; and if there is no other choice, give you tips on what to do with what's left over.

When you go shopping, remember not to get carried away with all the things you'd like to try and end up with more than you could ever eat. Set aside some thinking time when you plan what you are going to cook during the week. Check your storecupboard and make a shopping list before you hit the supermarket. And take advantage of the special offers only on things that you will use in good time.

Ready-mades

While on the subject of shopping, I will put in a quiet word for ready-made items. Jars of easy garlic and chilli are very useful to keep in the fridge as you can use just a small quantity, which is obviously just what you need when cooking for one. So in the recipes, I only use fresh garlic if you need a whole clove or more. If it suits you to buy other ready-mades, then go for it.

Batch bake to use your freezer

One crucial part of your kitchen armoury is, of course, the freezer; and I mean really using your freezer instead of just freezing things.

There are some freezer basics that I find indispensible. A pack of frozen peas is a great standby, as is a pack of diced onions, free-flow so you can just tip out what you need. The free-flow principle, or items wrapped and frozen individually, is essential. If you have never tried to separate one of the chicken breasts from a frozen pack of four and regretted the fact that you didn't separate them before you froze them, I'd be surprised. It's worth the few extra minutes it takes to put away the shopping, to make sure that food is ready in the right quantities when you need it.

Once you've cooked, always freeze the extras in individual portions ready to be thawed and re-heated.

Enjoy yourself

The key to keeping up a good habit is making it fun. If you loathe running a mile every morning, how long are you going to keep it up? So try not to make a chore of cooking – it doesn't have to be. Take your time in the food market or store and try out different things to keep your meals varied and interesting. Vary the recipes depending on what you have in the cupboard. Experiment!

I have included measurements for all the ingredients but I don't really expect you to measure 3 tbsp wine, that's just to give you an idea of how much you need – just pour some in the pan. So there's no need to ask 'how much is a dash of chilli sauce?' or 'a drizzle of salad dressing'. For you, it might be one shake of the bottle or four, one spoonful or several – it's really up to you.

Make it stylish

Finally, if you eat 'on the run' all the time, you'll lose the pleasure of enjoying your food, and then you won't be bothered to cook. It's a vicious circle to be avoided at all costs. So when you have taken the trouble to prepare your meal, make sure you set a place at the table, pour a glass of water or wine, sit down and take time over your food.

You may also like to impress others with your culinary skills, or let them impress you. Why not invite a friend or friends round for a regular supper? It doesn't have to be anything extra special but it will just give you that added incentive when you start to run out of steam. Don't let that happen when there are so many delicious things out there just waiting for you to enjoy.

Setting Up Your Kitchen

You don't need any special equipment for these recipes – your ordinary kitchen basics will be fine, so just use what you have. You hardly need me to list saucepans, measuring jug and mixing bowl. So here are just a few notes on things that might be particularly useful.

- Use whatever gadgets you like – anything that makes cooking easier or more enjoyable is fine.

- If you don't have a food processor or hand blender, I'd recommend you consider buying a little electric hand whisk and a hand-held blender – you can get them from the supermarket for a few pounds – to speed up whisking, puréeing and so on.

- You need a microwave only for the Microwave Meringues, and you don't need a slow-cooker or a pressure cooker – but you can use them if you like.

- I often bake cakes in a rectangular tin or a 900g loaf tin – much easier to divide and store. I also have some 13cm cake tins.

- Do remember to use your smaller oven if you have one.

- You can buy a small plastic, pump-action device to whip a small quantity of cream. Personally I prefer my miniature sauce whisk but I know people who love them. For measuring, I was given some plastic measuring cups with the calibration on the inside. They are so much easier to use than having to look at the outside of a jug.

- Match the quantity of food you are cooking to the size of the cooking pot. If it is too large, the food will cook too quickly and will dry out, or not cook through properly before the outside begins to burn. You may want to treat yourself to an individual ovenproof or flameproof dish.

- Make sure you have enough small saucepans. Before you rush out and buy the traditional set of small, medium and large, consider whether you may be better with two medium-sized saucepans and one small. You can always borrow a large one at Christmas. I also have a tiny 11cm saucepan. I like a fairly large wok – useful for stir-frying and general cooking – and a small omelette pan; if you cook on gas, make sure it balances on your hob.

Halogen ovens

I had never used a halogen oven before but it seemed a good idea for cooking in small quantities so I have tested some of the recipes in a halogen oven to compare the results and added a few notes on things I found more successful. I did find it particularly good for things like sausages that you might grill or oven cook. It's also much better than a microwave for defrosting and reheating.

I'm not sure I'm a convert yet – I'm so used to knowing how my oven cooks, and I found getting things in and out a bit awkward – but I can see why people might get hooked. They are certainly efficient and economical, especially for one.

There are a few principles you need to apply when converting ordinary recipes to cooking in the halogen oven.

- You may need some extra oven trays and other things that will fit inside the oven. I found that sturdy 23cm cake tins were a good size, and I used the base of a springform cake tin as a baking sheet.

- You need to get used to the fact that it is both an oven and a hob, so the top rack is more like a grill than the top of an oven; the bottom rack is the oven – so make sure you use the right section of the oven for the type of cooking you are doing.

- Preheat the oven to the required temperature before putting in the food.

- Wrapping in foil can help food cook through evenly but do make sure it is securely wrapped as the fan is quite strong.

- Everything cooks more quickly than in a conventional oven so reduce the cooking times by at least 20 per cent. Until you get used to it, I suggest you keep an eye on the food once half the cooking time has elapsed.

- It's useful for reheating portions – each one takes about 5 minutes in the preheated oven.

- For dedicated halogen recipes, take a look at Sarah Flower's *The Everyday Halogen Cookbook* and *Perfect Baking with Your Halogen Oven*.

Freezing

I have already extolled the virtues of the freezer in making life easier for singles, but remember not to put too much in at once, as it is better if you don't leave food in there too long.

- Always pack food well for the freezer. Use freezer-quality plastic bags or one-quantity freezer containers with secure or clip lids.

- Always label parcels with the contents and the date. There is no use thinking you will be able to recognise that fruit cake in three months' time – it is simply not going to happen – and what a disappointment when you defrost it thinking it's a beef casserole!

- Allow enough time for food to defrost either in the fridge or at room temperature, so take it out of the freezer the night before, or in the morning, so you can cook it for dinner.

- Always reheat food thoroughly until it is piping hot.

- Never refreeze food that has been defrosted.

A word on hygiene

I think if you use your common sense you can't go far wrong, even if you are new to the kitchen. Wash your hands before you cook; keep anything you've bought from a chill cabinet in the fridge; keep food well wrapped; keep an eye on use-by dates on perishable items; don't refreeze; don't reheat more than once; when reheating, make sure the food is piping hot right through. Simple!

CHAPTER 3

The Single's Storecupboard

A judicious choice of sensible stocks in your food cupboard will provide a sound basis for all your cooking, and you'll know you have some basic items when you cook and be able to rustle up a last-minute snack. Build up your list gradually as you cook the dishes and personalise it to what you like.

Dry goods
- Ground almonds
- Baking powder
- Bicarbonate of soda
- Plain chocolate, 70% cocoa or more
- Cocoa powder
- Cornflour
- Couscous
- Plain flour
- Rolled oats
- Rice, long-grain and risotto
- Pasta
- Sugar, caster and soft brown

Cans
- Baked beans
- Beans, mixed beans, borlotti or cannellini
- Chickpeas
- Custard
- Passata
- Pink or red salmon
- Tomatoes
- Tuna

Jars and bottles

- Balsamic vinegar
- Honey
- Lemon juice or lime juice (or you may prefer to keep a fresh lemon)
- Oil, olive and rapeseed, or another oil of your choice
- Pesto sauce
- Redcurrant jelly
- Wine
- Wine vinegar
- Worcestershire sauce

Spices and condiments

- Black peppercorns in a grinder
- Chilli powder or easy chilli
- Dijon mustard
- Dried herbs such as bay leaves, oregano, sage, thyme
- Garlic, easy garlic or garlic purée – the ready-made options are often easier than using fresh when you are only using small quantities but make your own choice
- Ginger, or a jar of ready-prepared shredded root ginger
- Sea salt
- Spices such as cumin, mixed spice, paprika
- Stock cubes, or home-made stock or stock pots – remember they are generally designed to make 300ml so don't use a whole cube for a small quantity
- Tomato purée or sundried tomato purée

Freezer

- Chicken breasts
- Diced onions, free-flow so you just tip out what you need
- Peas
- Peppers
- Prawns
- Puff pastry, cut into smaller portions
- Salmon steaks

Fresh

- Bacon
- Butter – I use unsalted butter, but I have only specified unsalted where I think it is essential; you should use a butter or a spread of your choice
- Carrots
- Cheese – a hard cheese with plenty of flavour is the most flexible cooking option, and you don't need as much to get a great taste
- Crème fraîche
- Eggs
- Garlic or use easy garlic
- Onions
- Parmesan cheese
- Potatoes
- Shallots

CHAPTER 4

Tips for Beginners

Many people who are cooking for themselves are not so experienced at working from cookery books, so here's a few notes to help you get the hang of it.

Using this book

- Each ingredients list gives the quantity, then the basic preparation, unless it's really obvious. For example, I'll list if you need to peel a potato because it's not always necessary but I'll assume you skin an onion.

- You don't have to measure exactly for most things.

- Fry over a medium heat unless the recipe says otherwise. Especially with few ingredients in the pan, they will burn if the heat is too high.

- Smell and taste food as you cook and make adjustments accordingly.

- No two ovens are the same and every dish will vary slightly when different people cook it. Check foods while you are cooking. Once you get used to your own oven you'll know if you have to make adjustments one way or another.

How do you know when it's done?

It got very boring repeating 10 minutes prep, 20 minutes cookng on almost every recipe but that's about right for most dishes. Check the times given for each stage, plus here's a quick guide to how to tell when things are ready.

- **Beef:** For slightly pink in the middle and rich brown on the outside, press it lightly and it should be tender.

- **Cakes:** The top should start to brown and the cake will start to shrink from the sides of the tin. Gently press the centre of the cake and it should spring back. For denser-textured cakes, put a skewer or sharp knife into the centre of the cake and it should come out clean.

- **Chicken:** Pierce the thickest part of the meat – that's the thigh on a whole chicken – and the juices should run clear, not pink. Avoid piercing it too often or you'll lose precious juices.

- **Green vegetables:** Better undercooked than soggy – pierce with a sharp knife and it should slide in easily but still feel firm and crunchy. Bite it to test!

- **Lamb:** Lamb should be browned on the outside and pink in the middle, and should feel tender, not spongy, when pressed.

- **Pasta:** They key words here are *al dente* – 'to the bite' – it should be just soft but not soggy, so still with a bit of bite.

- **Pork:** Like chicken, the juices should run clear. If you slow-cook pork, it will be so tender it will just pull apart.

- **Rice:** Similar to pasta – try a bit. It should be just tender enough to bite.

- **Root vegetables:** A sharp knife should slide into the vegetable easily.

What if it all goes wrong?

For ordinary, everyday cooking, if it tastes good, it is good. This is not about restaurant-quality presentation or Masterchef complexity, so don't worry too much about rights and wrongs; learn by mistakes and you'll soon grow in confidence. However, here are a few rescue remedies that could come in handy.

- **The sauce is too runny:** Remove the lid and simmer for a bit longer to evaporate some of the liquid and 'reduce' the sauce. Alternatively, blend 1 tsp cornflour with 1 tsp of water, whisk it into the sauce a drop at a time and simmer until thickened. Or blend 1 tsp cornflour with 1 tsp butter to make a 'roux', and whisk that into the sauce in the same way.

- **The sauce is too thick:** Add some more of the liquid you used for cooking, usually hot water or stock. Next time, cover the pan.

- **There's not much flavour:** Add some salt and pepper, or some more of the spices or herbs used in the dish. Try a dash of Worcestershire sauce, chilli sauce or tomato purée.

- **Only some of the ingredients are cooked:** Just cook until everything is done – it may not look perfect but it should taste okay. Next time, cut ingredients into even-sized pieces and put the ingredients into the dish in the right order so the ones that take longest go in first.

- **I've overcooked the vegetables:** Mix them and mash them with some butter and plenty of seasoning.

- **The dish is burnt on the base:** Never incorporate burnt food into the dish. Try to lift off the good stuff into a clean pan, add a little more liquid and reheat. Next time, cook over a lower heat, watch and stir.

- **It doesn't look very good:** Add a herb garnish, a knob of butter or a twist of black pepper, or accompany with a colourful side dish.

- **The cake has sunk in the middle:** So what? If you are serving to guests, serve it already sliced and sprinkled with icing sugar rubbed through a fine sieve or tea strainer. Next time, make sure the mixture is not too wet and that you have used the right size eggs. Most raw cake mixtures should be a 'dropping consistency', so they drop off the wooden spoon in nice lumps.

Conversion charts

This book provides metric measurements, but those who still prefer imperial, or who want to use US measures, can use these conversions.

If you use American cup measures, an American cup is 250ml of liquid, or whatever volume fits into the space, so the same weight of two different foods – butter and flour, for example – will have different cup measurements.

Weight

Metric	Imperial
25g	1oz
50g	2oz
75g	3oz
100g	4oz
150g	5oz
175g	6oz
200g	7oz
225g	8oz
250g	9oz
300g	10oz
350g	12oz
400g	14oz
450g	1lb

Liquid Measure

Metric	Imperial	US cup
5ml	1 tsp	1 tsp
15ml	1 tbsp	1 tbsp
50ml	2fl oz	3 tbsp
60ml	2½fl oz	¼ tbsp
75ml	3fl oz	⅓ cpup
100ml	4fl oz	scant ½ cup
125ml	4½fl oz	½ cup
150ml	5fl oz	⅔ cup
200ml	7fl oz	scant 1 cup
250ml	10fl oz	1 cup
300ml	½pt	1¼ cups
350ml	12fl oz	1⅓ cups
450ml	¾pt	1¾ cups
500ml	20fl oz	2 cups
600ml	1pt	2½ cups

Oven Temperatures

^{o}C	^{o}F
110°C	225°F
120°C	250°F
140°C	275°F
150°C	300°F
160°C	325°F
180°C	350°F
190°C	375°F
200°C	400°F
220°C	425°F
230°C	450°F
240°C	475°F

Measurements

Metric	Imperial
5cm	2in
10cm	4in
13cm	5in
15cm	6in
18cm	7in
20cm	8in
25cm	10in
30cm	12in

Soups and Snacks

Soups are brilliant foods when you are cooking for one. They are easy to make from whatever ingredients are in season or you have available, they clock up plenty of your five a day, you can freeze them, make them into a light snack or a full meal, serve them for lunch, supper or a snack.

It's not really worth making an individual portion of soup, so these recipes offer four servings, with ideas on different ways to serve, whether you decide to freeze them and spread out the portions, or put them in the fridge and stick with similar flavours for several days.

I think it is even more tempting to snack if you are on your own, so it follows that it is even more important to snack on healthy foods rather than high-fat crisps or sweet foods. Look at the ideas for light meals on page 42 and aim to have plenty of only healthy things in the cupboard – that makes it easier not to be tempted by too many things that should be reserved for treats.

Curried Apple Soup

Ingredients
1 tbsp oil
1 tbsp butter
2 shallots, finely chopped
2 tsp easy ginger root
1 tbsp korma curry paste
2 crisp eating apples,
    peeled, cored and cut into
    chunks
1 small potato, peeled and
    cut into chunks
1.2 litres chicken or
    vegetable stock
120ml milk
Salt and freshly ground black
    pepper

To garnish
Crème fraîche
A few fresh coriander leaves

This unusual and slightly retro combination actually works really well. It's a beautifully coloured soup, so ideal for wintry days. Use a good-quality curry paste and make the soup as hot as you like – this is just warming.

- Heat the oil and butter and fry the shallots for about 3 minutes until soft but not browned.

- Add the ginger and curry paste and stir in well.

- Stir in the apples, potato and stock, bring to the boil, then simmer for about 15 minutes until the potato is tender.

- Leave to cool slightly, then purée in a food processor or with a hand blender until smooth.

- Return to a clean pan, stir in the milk and season to taste with salt and pepper. Reheat gently without allowing the soup to boil.

- Serve with a spoonful of crème fraîche and a few coriander leaves in the bowl.

- Cool, then pour into a freezer container, label and freeze the extra portions without the crème fraîche or coriander.

Serving the remaining portions
- When you serve, try replacing the coriander with a spoonful of mango chutney, or some crumbled tortilla chips.

• Soups and Snacks

Chicken and Sweetcorn Chowder

A chowder is a rich and creamy soup made with potatoes, onions, bacon and milk and is ideal for a meal on its own. If you like, you can cut the kernels from 3 fresh corn cobs; I use canned to take away the hard work.

- Heat the oil and butter in a large pan, then fry the onion and bacon for about 3 minutes until soft but not browned.

- Add the potatoes and fry for 5 minutes, stirring, without allowing them to brown.

- Add the corn and stir everything together well. Add the stock, bring to the boil, then simmer for about 5 minutes until the potatoes are cooked.

- Stir in the milk, chicken and tarragon, then season to taste with salt and pepper and heat through over a low heat.

- Process half the soup in a food processor or with a hand blender until it has a coarse texture rather than a purée, then return it to the pan and reheat gently, if necessary.

- Serve garnished with tarragon leaves.

- Cool, then pour into a freezer container, label and freeze the extra portions.

Serving the remaining portions
- When you serve, try adding a spoonful of sherry to the soup; frying some chopped mushrooms to stir in; or grilling a bacon rasher until very crisp, then chopping it and sprinkling it on the top.

Ingredients
1 tbsp oil
1 tbsp butter
1 onion, finely chopped
2 rashers lean bacon, finely chopped
2 potatoes, peeled and diced
250g can of corn kernels, drained
600ml chicken stock
400ml milk
200g cooked chicken, finely chopped
2 tsp chopped fresh tarragon
Salt and freshly ground black pepper

To garnish
A few fresh tarragon leaves

Butter Bean and Bacon Soup

Ingredients
2 tbsp oil
1 onion, chopped
2 rashers lean bacon, chopped
2 carrots, chopped
1 celery stick, chopped
1 garlic clove, chopped
400g can of chopped tomatoes
600ml stock or water
1 tsp tomato purée
1 tsp dried oregano
400g can of butter beans, drained
Salt and freshly ground black pepper

To garnish
1 tbsp chopped fresh parsley

Pulses are a good source of protein, filling and inexpensive so are great for soups, as a side dish, to use in a casserole or to make a meat dish go further. You can soak then boil dried beans if you prefer but cans are very good.

- Heat the oil and fry the onion, bacon, carrots, celery and garlic for about 3 minutes until soft but not browned.

- Stir in the tomatoes, stock or water, tomato purée and oregano and bring to a gentle simmer. Continue to simmer for about 15 minutes until the soup is piping hot.

- Add the beans and simmer for 5 minutes.

- Season to taste with salt and pepper, then serve garnished with parsley.

- Cool, then pour into a freezer container, label and freeze the extra portions.

Variations
You can use almost any type of beans for this soup. Try it with borlotti, cannellini, chickpeas or red kidney beans. Taste the soup and add a dash of red wine, a sprinkling of paprika or other flavouring that you feel would suit the new ingredients.

Serving the remaining portions

- **Rice and Beans:** Cook 50g long-grain rice in a pan of boiling water for 5 minutes until almost cooked, then drain. Add to a portion of soup in a pan and simmer for about 5 minutes until hot and the rice is tender and has absorbed a little of the liquid. Serve with crusty wholemeal bread.

- **Brandied Bean and Bacon Soup:** Purée the soup – it will still be chunky. Reheat, adding 1 tsp brandy and a little boiling water if necessary. Stir in a spoonful of crème fraîche and some chopped fresh parsley to serve.

- **Bacon and Bean Cobbler:** Rub 1 tbsp butter and 1 tbsp lard into 4 tbsp plain flour and ¼ tsp baking powder, then mix to a dough with about 1 tbsp water. Put the soup in an ovenproof dish or pudding basin. Shape the topping into a circle and mark into quarters. Pop on top of the soup and bake in a preheated oven at 200°C/Gas 6 for 20 minutes until the cobbler is cooked and the soup piping hot.

Carrot and Coriander Soup

Ingredients

2 tbsp oil
1 onion, finely chopped
1 garlic clove, chopped
1 celery stick, chopped
1 tsp coriander seeds,
    crushed
1 potato, peeled and
    chopped
500g carrots, chopped
1 litre vegetable or chicken
    stock
2 tbsp tomato purée
Salt and freshly ground black
    pepper

To garnish

2 tbsp chopped fresh
    coriander
A spoonful of crème fraîche

Coriander perfectly complements the slight sweetness of the carrots, which also impart that lovely rich colour. It's worth setting the table and sitting down properly to your meal as you will appreciate it all the more.

- Heat the oil and fry the onion, garlic, celery and crushed coriander seeds for about 3 minutes until the onion is soft but not browned.

- Add the potato and carrots, pour in the stock and bring to the boil.

- Stir in the tomato purée and season with salt and pepper. Simmer for about 20 minutes until the vegetables are very tender.

- Purée until smooth in a food processor or with a hand blender, adding most of the fresh coriander at the same time.

- Return the soup to the pan to heat through gently, then serve garnished with a swirl of crème fraîche and the remaining coriander.

- Cool, then pour into a freezer container, label and freeze the extra portions without the crème fraîche.

Serving the remaining portions

- **Hot Carrot Soup:** Reheat with 1 tsp hot chilli sauce – or more if you like things spicy – and sprinkle a few slightly broken tortilla chips on top.

- **Carrot Soup with Mango Chutney:** Serve with 1 tbsp mango chutney for garnish and strips of naan bread or toasted pitta bread.

- **Carrot Soup with Tomato Bread:** You can also serve it with tomato bread or fresh crusty rolls.

Chilled Almond Soup

This is an Andalusian dish. It has a wonderful flavour and is easy to make for one or in a larger quantity as an elegant starter for dinner with friends. Traditionally it is made by grinding almonds by hand, but I cheat.

Ingredients
25g ground almonds
½ tsp easy garlic
2 tbsp fresh breadcrumbs
Salt
2 tbsp olive oil
½ tsp wine vinegar
300ml water

To serve
Ice cubes
100g black grapes

- Put the almonds, garlic, breadcrumbs and a pinch of salt in a food processor.

- Pour in the oil and process to a paste.

- Switch on the processor. Add the wine vinegar to the water, then pour it into the almond mixture. Season to taste with salt.

- Pour into your bowl, float the ice cubes in the soup and garnish with the grapes.

Makes 4 servings

Traditional Vegetable Soup

Ingredients
2 tbsp olive oil
1 onion, finely chopped
1 garlic clove, crushed
1 celery stick, sliced or diced
2 carrots, sliced or diced
1 turnip, sliced or diced
1 parsnip, sliced or diced
1.2 litres vegetable stock
100ml passata
1 tsp dried mixed herbs
Salt and freshly ground black
   pepper

To garnish
A handful of chopped fresh
   parsley

There's no need to weigh anything for this soup, just throw in whichever vegetables you have to hand – great for making use of a glut or taking advantage of special offers. Don't use too many strongly flavoured vegetables.

- Heat the oil and fry the onion, garlic and celery for about 3 minutes until soft but not browned.

- Add the carrots, turnip and parsnip, or vegetables of your choice, cut into even-sized pieces. Add the stock, passata and herbs and season with salt and pepper. Bring to the boil, then simmer for about 20 minutes until the vegetables are tender.

- Serve garnished with parsley.

- Cool, then pour into a freezer container, label and freeze the extra portions.

Variations
Vary the vegetables you use to make a whole range of delicious soups. For a Celery Soup, use 6 celery sticks and a large potato. Pairing vegetables also works well. Try potato with parsnip, beetroot, carrot or celariac. Vary the herbs for a variety of flavours. You can add pulses, too, to create a more robust soup.

Serving the remaining portions

- **Cream of Vegetable Soup:** Purée the soup until smooth in a food processor or with a hand blender, then tip into a pan and heat through with 1 tbsp double cream.

- **Vegetable Soup with Pasta and Pesto:** Bring a small pan of water to the boil, throw in a small handful of soup pasta – the tiny stars – return to the boil and boil for 4 minutes, then drain well. Meanwhile, purée the soup (as above) or leave it as it is. Place it in a pan and stir through 1 tbsp pesto and the drained pasta and heat through. Add a little extra water or stock if necessary.

- **Thick Vegetable and Bean Soup with Garlic Croûtons:** This should make two portions. Purée the soup (as above) and return it to the pan. Add 1 small rinsed and drained can of mixed, borlotti or cannelloni beans, bring to the boil, then simmer for 3 minutes until the soup is piping hot. Season to taste with salt and pepper and add a little water or stock if necessary. Meanwhile, make some croûtons to serve with the soup. Dice thickly sliced bread, then fry in hot oil until golden and crisp; or toss in oil and grill or flash in a hot oven; or simply toast then dice the bread.

Beetroot and Brie Toasts

Ingredients
2–4 slices granary bread
4–8 slices cooked beetroot
4–8 slices Brie
Salt and freshly ground black
  pepper

To serve
Squeeze of lemon juice
Rocket and watercress salad

If you buy fresh uncooked beetroot, trim the stalks to about 2.5cm and boil for about 1½ hours until tender before trimming and slipping off the skins … or you can buy vacuum-packed fresh cooked beetroot.

- Toast one side of the bread, then turn it over.

- Arrange the beetroot slices on top, then cover with the cheese and season with salt and pepper.

- Place under a hot grill for about 5 minutes until hot and the cheese is melting.

- Squeeze a little lemon juice over the top and serve with a rocket and watercress salad.

Variations
Try using a blue cheese in this recipe, such as gorgonzola, Danish blue or Stilton. Alternatively, if you prefer a milder version, opt for a Cheddar, Gouda or Mozzarella. You could dice or grate the beetroot if you prefer, in which case you could mix it with some finely grated raw carrot. If you have some fresh herbs available, sprinkle them over the top before you serve the dish.

• Soups and Snacks

Using the remaining cheese and beetroot

- If you have some cheese left over; use the rest for Caramelised Onion and Goats' Cheese Puffs (page 38), or in a ' Cheese Salad (page 138) substituting the Brie for the goats' chese.

- **Sliced Beetroot with Crème Fraîche and Pepper:** Slice some of the beetroot and heat for a few minutes in the microwave, then serve as a vegetable with grilled meat or chicken, perhaps with a spoonful of crème fraîche and plenty of black pepper.

- **Marmalade Beetroot:** Dice a serving of beetroot and place in a small pan with 1 tbsp butter, 1 tbsp finely chopped marmalade, and 2 tbsp orange juice. Heat, tossing occasionally, until most of the liquid has evaporated.

- **Beetroot with Lemon:** Grate raw, peeled beetroot, toss in hot butter in a pan for 2 minutes, then dress with lemon juice and black pepper.

- **Beetroot Soup:** Mash or purée a portion of cooked beetroot with 1 tbsp lemon juice, 1 tbsp honey, a pinch of salt and plenty of freshly ground black pepper. Add enough water to make a soup consistency and serve hot or cold with a spoonful of soured cream.

- **Old English Beetroot Cake:** Try it – it may surprise you (page 174).

Spinach and Avocado Salad with Pancetta

Ingredients
1–2 slices pancetta
2 handfuls of baby spinach
½–1 small avocado
1 tbsp lemon juice
50g Parmesan cheese,
  shaved into slivers
Salt and freshly ground black
  pepper

For the balsamic vinaigrette
1 tbsp olive oil
1 tsp balsamic vinegar
½ tsp Dijon mustard

A bag of baby spinach only needs washing to give you the basis of a delicious salad. A few leaves of rocket will add that delicious, slightly peppery taste. You can make a larger quantity of the dressing and keep it in the fridge.

- Grill the pancetta until crisp, then chop roughly.

- Arrange the spinach on a plate.

- Peel and stone the avocado, slice into crescents and toss lightly in the lemon juice. Arrange on top of the spinach.

- Sprinkle with the Parmesan shavings and season with salt and pepper.

- Whisk together the dressing ingredients and drizzle a little over the salad. Sprinkle with the pancetta before serving.

Using the remaining spinach and avocado
- **Spinach:** Use any remaining spinach as a vegetable, for Lamb Cutlets with Sweet Spinach (page 81), Chicken and Avocado Salad (page 102) or Minted Chicken Salad (page 114).

- **Avocado:** If you only want half the avocado, do not peel the second half. Brush with lemon juice and seal tightly in clingfilm. Store in the fridge and use quickly in Chicken and Avocado Salad (page 102) or as a simple starter.

Asparagus with Poached Eggs and Parmesan

Indulge yourself when asparagus is in season. In an asparagus pan, the stems are immersed in water while the tender tips cook in the steam. If you don't have an asparagus pan, wrap a piece of foil around the stems to keep them upright.

- Half fill a deep pan with water and bring to the boil.

- Meanwhile, bring another small pan of water to the boil.

- Place the asparagus in the deep pan, ideally with the tips above the water, cover and cook for about 4 minutes, depending on size, until just tender.

- While they are cooking, break the egg into a cup, then carefully pour the egg into the boiling water in the second pan, stirring around the egg white to coalesce. Cook for 2–3 minutes.

- Drain the asparagus and place on a serving plate. Top with the butter, then place the poached egg on top. Sprinkle with the Parmesan and a good grinding of black pepper.

Ingredients
4 large or 8 small asparagus
spears
25g unsalted butter
1 egg
25g Parmesan cheese
shavings
Freshly ground black
pepper

Makes 1 serving

Caramelised Onion and Goats' Cheese Puffs

Ingredients

125g puff pastry, at room temperature
6 tbsp caramelised onion chutney
75g goats' cheese, sliced

To serve

Mixed leaf salad
Balsamic Dressing (page 139)

Best served warm or at room temperature, you can make this in any shape or size. If you've read the introduction to this book, you'll have quartered your 500g pack of puff pastry before you put it in the freezer so just defrost one chunk.

- Heat the oven to 200°C/Gas 6 and grease some cake pans, Yorkshire pudding pans or a baking sheet, and put another baking sheet in the oven to heat.

- Roll out the pastry thinly on a lightly floured surface. Either cut into shapes to line the tins, or place on the baking sheet. Moisten the edges and roll them in slightly to create an edge on the pastry to stop the chutney spreading. Prick the bases with a fork.

- Fill the cases with the chutney and top with slices of cheese.

- Place the tray of puffs on the hot baking tray and bake in the oven for about 10 minutes until risen and cooked through.

- Serve with some salad leaves drizzled with balsamic vinegar and olive oil.

Using the remaining goats' cheese
You will probably use about half a 150g roll of goats' cheese. Use the rest for a Watercress and Goats' Cheese Salad (page 138) or substitute goats' cheese for Brie in Beetroot and Brie Toasts (page 34) or just grill it on toast.

Makes 1 serving

Quick Oriental Prawn Noodles

Free-flow frozen raw prawns are ideal as you can tip out what you need in the morning to defrost in the fridge during the day. A block of noodles from a 500g packet weighs about 80–100g, which is a generous portion.

- Heat the oil in a wok or pan and fry the shallots and pepper over a medium heat for 3 minutes until soft but not browned.

- Bring a pan of lightly salted water to the boil, add the noodles and boil for 2 minutes until soft. Drain well.

- Meanwhile, mix together the honey, tomato purée, hoisin sauce, wine vinegar and Dijon mustard. Stir into the pan and mix well.

- Stir in the prawns and cook, stirring, for a few minutes until they turn pink, adding a little boiling water, if necessary, to keep everything moist.

- Stir in the noodles and toss together well to warm through. Taste, and season with salt and pepper, if necessary, and serve garnished with the spring onion.

Ingredients
1 tbsp oil
4 shallots, thinly sliced
1 red pepper, thinly sliced
Salt and freshly ground
  black pepper
½–1 block egg noodles
1 tbsp honey
1 tbsp tomato purée
1 tbsp hoisin sauce
½ tsp white wine vinegar
1 tsp Dijon mustard
125g raw peeled prawns
1 spring onion, shredded

Stilton Pâté

Ingredients
50g Stilton cheese, crumbled
1 tbsp butter
1 tsp brandy (optional)
2 tsp cream cheese
1 tbsp chopped walnuts
A little milk
Salt and freshly ground black
   pepper (optional)

To serve
Crackers
Crusty bread and salad

This makes a tasty light meal served with crackers, or with bread and salad to make it more substantial. The quantities don't really matter – just mash together the ingredients until you get a texture you like. Any crumbly cheese will work.

- Mash the Stilton lightly in a bowl, then mash in the butter.

- Stir in the brandy, if using, then the cream cheese and walnuts.

- Check the consistency and add a little milk if it is too firm, or a little more cheese if it feels too soft. It's entirely up to you to make it how you like it.

- Taste and season with salt and pepper if you wish. Stilton is slightly salty so it may not be necessary.

- Serve with crackers or crusty bread and salad.

Makes 4 servings

Garlic and Caramelised Pepper Bruschetta

This makes four portions of the caramelised peppers as it's a bit of a waste of time to do less, but they are great to use in other ways. This is a good dish for the halogen oven.

- Heat the oven to 200°C/Gas 6.

- Spread the peppers and onion in a baking tin, add 5 of the garlic cloves and season with salt and pepper.

- Whisk together the oil, sugar and balsamic vinegar, sprinkle over the vegetables, then toss together to coat. Roast in the oven for 35 minutes, stirring occasionally, until tender and well browned.

- Toast the rolls on both sides.

- Rub the remaining garlic clove over the inside surface of the rolls, squeezing the juice into the bread.Rub the tomato over the bread, again squeezing in the juice.

- Top with caramelised peppers and season with salt and pepper. Serve at room temperature or flash under the grill to serve hot.

- Put the remaining caramelised peppers in a screw-topped jar and store in the fridge.

Using the remaining peppers

- **Caramelised Peppers with Couscous:** Stir a portion of peppers through some couscous (page 52) and serve with salad.

- **Pasta with Caramelised Peppers and Cheese:** Stir about 100g cream cheese and a generous spoonful of the peppers through hot cooked pasta, and season with black pepper.

- **Steak Sandwich with Caramelised Peppers:** Flash-fry a minute steak, then sandwich in a roll with a portion of the peppers, a spoonful of hot tomato salsa and a dollop of mayonnaise.

Ingredients
4 large peppers of different colours, sliced
1 large red onion, thinly sliced
6 garlic cloves
Salt and freshly ground black pepper
3 tbsp oil
1 tbsp sugar
1 tsp balsamic vinegar
1–2 ciabatta rolls, sliced in half
1 ripe tomato, halved

Makes 4 servings

Ideas for Light Meals

Ideas for Ingredients
Any vegetables
Salad ingredients
Cold meats
Fancy breads
Pickles

You don't need full recipes for quick ideas, so keep these hints in mind when you are shopping, or when you need a little something in between meals or at the end of the day.

Fruit and nuts

- Why not buy a different fruit every time you go shopping and see if some of the more exotic options suit your taste.

- Remember that if you buy local fruit in season it will have the best flavour, so if you live in the UK, don't go looking for a perfect Cox's apple in February.

- There are plenty of individual packets of dried fruits, like mango and pineapple, which are absolutely delicious. Cheaper options are a handful of raisins, apricots or sultanas from a bigger packet. They make a great snack, but be aware that they are high in sugar.

- Nuts are also highly nutritious but high in fat and calories, so make them an occasional nibble.

Make a quick salad

- Grate a carrot and an apple and toss in lemon juice.

- Small cans of sardines, smoked fish or tuna are ideal for topping a selection of salad leaves with sliced spring onions and tomatoes.

Beans on toast

- Add a dash of Worcestershire sauce to the beans.

- Toast some cheese on the bread before topping with the beans.

- Add a slice of ham or some crisp bacon to the plate.

- Top the lot with a poached or fried egg.

• *Soups and Snacks*

Omelettes

- Whisk a couple of eggs with some salt and pepper and a dash of milk. Melt a little butter in a small pan, preferably an omelette pan, add the egg and swirl it around to cover the base, lifting the sides as it cooks to let the egg run underneath. When it is set and golden underneath and cooked but slightly soft on top, fold it in half and slide on to the plate. If you prefer it golden on both sides, slide the flat omelette out on to a plate, then invert it back into the pan to finish cooking the other side.

- Before you fold it, sprinkle in some grated cheese, chopped ham, cooked prawns, slivers of smoked salmon or diced cooked mushrooms.

Perfect pasta

Since you can cook pasta quickly in any quantity, make yourself a small bowl when you don't want a full-blown meal.

- **Pesto and Parmesan Pasta:** Stir through a spoonful of pesto sauce and sprinkle with Parmesan shavings.

- **Cheese and Herb Pasta:** Toss with a few spoonfuls of cream cheese, lots of black pepper and some chopped fresh herbs.

- **Tomato and Chilli Pasta:** Spice it up with a little passata or chopped tomatoes and a dash of chilli sauce.

Seafood

Quick to cook, healthy and arriving in the perfect portion size, what could be better than making fish a regular item on your menu? Plus there's so much variety that you can ring the changes almost endlessly. Remember that the delicate texture of fish needs to be treated gently otherwise it will spoil.

Many suppliers are now favouring species that are sustainably managed, and you can find out the latest information, including which fish fall into the categories one to five – from sustainable to unsustainable – at www.fishonline.org.

Cooking and Serving Fish

Category A sustainable fish
Atlantic salmon
Herring
Mussels
Rainbow trout
Tiger prawns

Category B sustainable fish
Albacore tuna
Coley
Dab
Dorado
Dover sole
Gurnard
Haddock
Halibut
Lemon sole
Pollock
Red mullet
Sardines
Scallop
Seabass
Seabream
Squid
Swordfish

Often the best way to serve fish is very simply, allowing it to show off its delicate textures and flavours; why bother with complicated recipes when you can serve a simple dish of grilled fish with fresh seasonal vegetables.

Cooking fish

- **Timing:** Times are approximate and depend on the thickness of the fish. Fish is ready when the flesh flakes easily with a fork.

- **Grilling:** Brush with oil and grill under a moderate grill for about 6 minutes each side. You can lay the fish on a piece of foil if it is likely to flake through the grill.

- **Frying:** Keep the heat to medium. You can protect delicate fish with a coating of seasoned flour, egg and breadcrumbs or batter before you cook for about 5 minutes each side.

- **Poaching:** Immerse the fish in stock or milk and simmer gently for around 15 minutes, then drain well, using the stock for a sauce rather than wasting it.

- **Oven-baking:** Best for whole fish, slash the sides and bake at 180°C/Gas 4 for about 20 minutes until browned and crisp.

Sauces and butters

- **Flavoured Mayonnaise:** Blend ½ tsp easy garlic into 150ml mayonnaise; or beat in some chopped fresh herbs, such as parsley or dill. There is a mayonnaise recipe on page 139.

- **White Sauce:** Whisk 1 tsp cornflour and 1 tsp butter into 150ml milk and season with salt and pepper. Bring to the boil then simmer, stirring, for 3 minutes until thickened.

- **Parsley Sauce:** Stir 1 tbsp chopped parsley into a White Sauce.

- **Tartare Sauce:** Chop 1 shallot, 1 tsp capers, 1 small cornichon and stir into 150ml mayonnaise with a squeeze of lemon juice.

• Seafood

Crab Balls with Dipping Sauces

These crab balls can be eaten hot or cold, so you can make a meal of them or a snack. Make your own breadcrumbs in the processor, or you can buy tubs of breadcrumbs (but not those packs of bright orange crumbs!).

- While the crabmeat drains, chop one spring onion and slice the other.

- Mix the crabmeat with the chopped spring onion, the parsley, lemongrass, 3 tbsp of the breadcrumbs and half the egg. Season with salt and pepper.

- Using floured hands to prevent the mixture sticking, roll the mixture into small balls about the size of a golf ball. Put in the fridge for a few minutes to cool and firm.

- Place the remaining flour, egg and breadcrumbs on 3 plates. Roll the balls in the flour, then the egg, then the breadcrumbs.

- Heat the oil and fry the crab balls for about 5–8 minutes, turning until they are golden on all sides.

- Garnish with the remaining spring onion and serve with salad and dipping sauces.

Ingredients
170g can of crabmeat, drained
2 spring onions
2 tsp chopped fresh parsley
¼ tsp easy lemongrass
60g breadcrumbs
1 egg, beaten
Salt and freshly ground black pepper
2 tbsp plain flour (optional)
3 tbsp olive oil

To serve
Chilli, lemon and hoisin dipping sauces
Mixed salad

Prawns in Lime and Chilli Marinade

Ingredients
1 tbsp lime juice
½ tbsp soy sauce
½ tsp easy ginger root
¼ tsp easy garlic
¼ tsp chilli sauce
100g raw prawns
1 spring onion, shredded

To serve
Egg noodles
Green salad

It takes no time at all to thread some food onto a kebab skewer but it somehow makes the meal you serve up so much more interesting! Soak wooden skewers before use so they do not char. This marinade is also good with chicken.

- Whisk together the lime juice, soy sauce, ginger, garlic and chilli. Add the prawns and leave to marinate for at least an hour.

- Thread the prawns onto soaked wooden skewers and grill for about 6 minutes, turning and basting with the marinade, until pink and succulent.

- Garnish with the spring onion and serve with egg noodles and a green salad.

Pan-fried Scallops with Prawns

Cook scallops for a short time otherwise they will go rubbery and taste of nothing much. Cooked quickly in hot butter, they are delicious. Some people don't like frozen scallops but – in the absence of perfection – they can taste pretty good!

- Heat the oil and butter in a griddle or frying pan over a medium-high heat. Fry the courgette quickly until soft and golden.

- Add the scallops and prawns and continue to cook for about 4 minutes, tossing in the butter until the prawns are pink and the scallops lightly golden.

- Squeeze over the lemon juice and season with salt and pepper.

- Arrange the watercress on a plate with the bread and butter and lemon wedges on the side. Spoon the seafood on top and serve at once.

Ingredients
1 tsp olive oil
1 tbsp butter
½ courgette, sliced
8 scallops
8 large, shell-on prawns
1 tbsp lemon juice
Salt and freshly ground
   black pepper

To serve
Handful of watercress
Lemon wedges
Brown bread and butter

Paprika Seafood and Artichokes

Ingredients
4 tbsp plain yoghurt
1 tsp easy garlic
½ finger chilli, chopped, or
    ¼ tsp easy chilli
¼ tsp paprika
Pinch of chilli powder
Salt and freshly ground black
    pepper
12 large raw prawns
½ x 400g can of artichoke
    hearts, drained and halved

To serve
Green salad
Crusty bread

I like prawns and they are very convenient for one, but you can use any firm-fleshed fish or seafood for this simple dish. You won't need all the artichokes but it is worth grilling them all together, then they are ready to use.

- Mix the yoghurt, garlic, chilli, paprika, chilli powder, salt and pepper. Add the prawns, stir well to cover, and marinate for at least an hour.

- If you have a griddle, griddle the artichoke hearts in the hot pan for a few minutes so you have lovely charred stripes across them.

- Add the prawns to the griddle and cook for about 8 minutes, turning and basting with the marinade, until they turn pink.

- Serve on a green salad with plenty of crusty bread.

Using the remaining artichoke hearts
- Use the remaining articokes in Farm Sausages with Roasted Vegetables (page 96) or simply toss them in a Vinaigrette Dressing (page 139) with a dash of chilli oil and loads of pepper and serve them as a starter with crusty bread and cold meats.

• Seafood

Seafood Chive Pancakes

You can make pancakes for this recipe, keep some in the freezer, or buy ready-made if you are short of time on another day. Use any combination of seafood. You really only then need a fresh salad, made with whatever you fancy, to complete the meal.

- Heat the butter and fry the shallot and garlic for 3 minutes until soft.

- Stir in the wine, then the flour and whisk to blend, then whisk in the milk, tomato purée and chives. Add the seafood and simmer gently for 5 minutes until the fish flakes and the sauce is thick. Season with salt and pepper.

- Place the pancakes in a serving dish, spoon in the mixture, then fold the pancakes over to enclose.

- Garnish with the tomatoes and serve with salad.

Ingredients
1 tbsp butter
1 shallot, finely chopped
½ tsp easy garlic
1 tbsp white wine
2 tsp plain flour
150ml milk
1 tsp tomato purée
1 tsp snipped fresh chives
100g mixed seafood, such
    as chunks of fish, prawns
    or scallops
Salt and freshly ground
    black pepper
2 Pancakes (page 142)

To serve
2 plum tomatoes
Mixed salad

Grilled Mackerel with Harissa Couscous

Ingredients

1 mackerel
1 lime
2 tbsp olive oil
2 shallots, thinly sliced
1 tsp harissa
4 tbsp couscous, toasted
100ml chicken stock
1 tbsp chopped fresh
   coriander
Salt and freshly ground black
   pepper

Mackerel are hugely under-rated. A strongly flavoured fish with a lovely texture, it's also very inexpensive and just the right size for one. Ask at the fish counter if they will bone the fish for you.

- Place the mackerel fillets in a small shallow dish.

- Halve the lime and seal half in clingfilm to use in another recipe. Cut a wedge off the remaining half, then squeeze the juice and grate the zest over the mackerel. Leave to marinate for about 15 minutes.

- Heat 1 tbsp of the oil in a pan and fry the shallots for 2 minutes.

- Stir in the harissa, then stir in the couscous until everything is well blended. Remove from the heat.

- Bring the stock to the boil, pour over the couscous and stir well. Cover and leave to stand.

- Lift the mackerel from the lime juice, sprinkle with the remaining oil and cook in a griddle pan or under the grill for about 5 minutes each side until cooked and with crisp skin.

- Scrape any remaining marinade into the couscous with the coriander and season with salt and pepper. Fluff up the grains with a fork.

- Pile the couscous onto the plate, top with the mackerel and serve garnished with the lime wedge.

Poached Fish with Sweet Potato

- Put the sweet potato in a small pan, cover with water, bring to the boil and simmer for about 10 minutes until tender.

- In a separate pan, place the fish, milk, garlic, shallot and peppercorns. Reserve 2 tbsp of the herbs and add the rest to the fish. Bring to a gentle simmer, cover and simmer gently for 8 minutes until the fish flakes easily. Lift out the fish, remove the skin, then put the flesh in a shallow ovenproof dish.

- Drain the potato, returning the hot water to the pan, then mash with just over half the butter and plenty of salt and pepper. Add the broccoli to the hot water, return to the boil, and simmer for a few minutes until just tender, then drain.

- Strain the fish cooking liquid and return it to the pan; make up to 200ml, if necessary, with a little more milk. Whisk in the cornflour and the remaining butter and bring to a simmer, stirring, then cook for 3 minutes until thick and smooth, stirring continuously.

- Stir in the remaining dill or parsley and season with salt and pepper. Pour over the fish, then top with the mash. Flash under a hot grill to brown the top, then serve with the broccoli.

Other ways with poached fish

- **Fish Pie:** Replace the sweet potato mash with traditional mashed potatoes and add some roughly chopped hard-boiled eggs and cooked, peeled prawns to the fish in its sauce. Assemble the pie and bake in a preheated oven at 200°C/Gas 6 for 15 minutes until heated through and golden on top.

- **Fish Pasta:** Make a White Sauce (page 46), then stir in 1 tbsp tomato purée and a portion of flaked poached fish. Cook a portion of pasta until *al dente*, then drain and mix with the sauce.

- **Fish Cakes:** Substitute poached fish for the salmon in Salmon Fish Balls (page 56) and serve with salad and chips.

Ingredients
1 small sweet potato, peeled and diced
1 pollock fillet
300ml milk
1 garlic clove
1 shallot
A few black peppercorns
2 sprigs of fresh dill or parsley, chopped
2–3 tbsp butter
Salt and freshly ground black pepper
A few broccoli florets
2 tsp cornflour

Salmon with Herb and Garlic Mayonnaise

Ingredients
1 salmon steak
2 tsp butter
Salt and freshly ground black
  pepper
150ml Mayonnaise (page
  139)
½ tsp easy garlic, or to taste
1 tbsp chopped fresh
  coriander

To serve
Minted baby new potatoes
Steamed green beans

Use salmon steaks or fillets for this simple dish. The garlic mayonnaise can be used to accompany almost anything, from steak to chicken, or used as a dip with grissini or cruditées, or as a salad dressing.

- Brush the steak with butter and season with salt and pepper.

- Cook under a hot grill for about 8 minutes each side until cooked through and the skin is crisp and golden.

- Blend the garlic into the mayonnaise and season with salt and pepper. Blend in the coriander to taste.

- Serve the fish and mayonnaise with boiled new potatoes tossed in butter and chopped fresh mint, and steamed green beans.

• Seafood

Thai-style Salmon

You can treat almost any robust fish in this way. I didn't list chilli dipping sauce in the storecupboard but it can be very useful to add to oriental-style sauces, to serve on the side of plain dishes, or as a dip with prawn crackers.

- Mix the chilli, soy and fish sauce in a shallow bowl, add the lime leaves and sesame oil and whisk together. Add the salmon and coat in the mixture. Leave to marinate for an hour or so if possible.

- Lift the fish out of the marinade and cook under a hot grill for about 8 minutes each side until cooked through with crispy skin, basting with the marinade as it cooks.

- Garnish the fish with the spring onion and serve with sticky rice, prawn crackers and a little more chilli dipping sauce.

Ingredients
1 tbsp chilli dipping sauce
1 tbsp soy sauce
½ tbsp Thai fish sauce
½ tsp crushed kaffir lime leaves
½ tsp sesame oil
1 salmon steak

To serve
1 spring onion, shredded
Sticky rice
Prawn crackers
Chilli dipping sauce

Salmon Fish Balls with Chunky Sauté Chips

You can also make this tasty dish with tuna, especially if you have opened a can for another recipe, or you have used a little in your lunchtime sandwiches. You could serve this with new potatoes if you prefer.

Ingredients
2 floury potatoes, peeled and diced
1 tbsp butter
Salt and freshly ground black pepper
1 salmon steak
1 tbsp chopped fresh dill
2 tsp lemon juice
1 tbsp plain flour
3 tbsp oil
1 egg, lightly beaten
75g breadcrumbs

For the chips
1 large potato, cut into thick chips
4 tbsp oil

To serve
Green beans or mushy peas

- Bring the potatoes to the boil in a pan of salted water and boil for 5 minutes until tender, then drain well.

- Mash with the butter, salt and pepper.

- Meanwhile grill the salmon under a medium grill for about 10 minutes until cooked through. Remove the skin and flake the fish then stir the salmon, dill and lemon juice into the potatoes. Leave to cool.

- Put the chips in a pan of salted water, bring to the boil, then simmer for 3 minutes. Drain well.

- With floured hands, shape the fish mixture into little balls about the size of golf balls and roll them in flour.

- Heat the oil in a large frying pan.

- Toss the fish balls in the egg, then the breadcrumbs, making sure they are well covered.

- Add the fish balls to the hot oil on one side of the pan and start to fry for about 8 minutes, turning to brown on all sides. Add the chips to the other side of the pan and fry until golden.

- Drain on kitchen paper and serve with green beans or peas.

Sea Bream with Minted Salsa Verde

You can also make this with seabass or other fish, in fact, as salsa verde goes well with most fish. Some people like to make it with basil instead of mint, or you could even add a touch of chilli to give it a bit more heat.

- Heat the oven to 190°C/Gas 5 and lightly oil a baking sheet.

- Make three or four deep slashes diagonally across one side of the fish and place it on the prepared sheet. Brush the top side with the remaining oil.

- Coarsely crush the breadcrumbs, wine vinegar, mint, anchovies, capers and garlic in a mortar and pestle. Beat in the oil and season with salt and pepper.

- Press a spoonful of the salsa into each of the slashes on the fish spreading the rest over the fish. Place in the oven to cook for 15 minutes until golden and the skin is crispy on the edges.

- Serve the fish with boiled rice or new potatoes.

Ingredients
1 tbsp olive oil
1 sea bream

For the salsa verde
15g breadcrumbs
½ tbsp red wine vinegar
A few fresh mint leaves
2 anchovies
½ tsp capers
½ tsp easy garlic
40ml olive oil
Salt and freshly ground
  black pepper

To serve
Boiled rice or new potatoes

Griddled Sole with Lemon Butter Sauce

Ingredients

1 tbsp plain flour
Salt and freshly ground black
  pepper
2 lemon sole fillets
1 tbsp olive oil
3 tbsp unsalted butter
2 tbsp white wine
3 tbsp double cream
1 tbsp lemon juice
½ tbsp chopped fresh
  parsley

To serve
Sauté potatoes
A fresh green vegetable

I think this kind of fish needs a very simple presentation and this light, delicate sauce is perfect. Make sure you keep your meals colourful as well as balancing flavours – here there's a lovely contrast of white and green.

- Season the flour with a little salt and pepper. Dip the fish in the flour.

- Heat the oil with 1 tbsp of the butter and fry the sole for about 4 minutes on each side until flaky and cooked through.

- Meanwhile, put the wine in a small pan and boil until reduced by half. Whisk in the remaining butter, then the cream and simmer for a few minutes, stirring occasionally.

- Add the lemon juice and parsley, whisking continuously, and season with salt and pepper.

- Pour the sauce over the fish, garnish with the parsley and serve with sauté potatoes and a green vegetable.

Makes 1 serving

Niçoise Salad

Recipes become classics for good reason – they encapsulate a superb combination of flavours and textures. This classic French recipe is one such example. Fortunately, it is also ideal for making in single – but generous – portions.

- Make the salad by tossing the ingredients together.

- Whisk the dressing ingredients together and season with salt and pepper.

- Pour the dressing over the salad and toss gently.

Using the remaining tuna
- Use in salads (page 138), with pasta (page 43), instead of the salmon in Salmon Fish Balls with Chunky Sauté Chips (page 56), or serve with salad and mayonnaise in sandwiches.

Variations
- Substitute a different selection of ingredients if you don't have everything to hand. It may not be an authentic Niçoise but if it is tasty, it really doesn't matter.

Ingredients

For the salad
100g can of tuna, flaked
4 boiled baby new potatoes
1 tomato, cut into chunks
1 shallot, finely chopped
1 hard-boiled egg, cut into chunks
1 anchovy fillet, finely chopped
A few lettuce leaves
A few cooked green beans
A few stoned black olives

For the dressing
15ml olive oil
Dash of Dijon mustard
¼ tbsp white wine vinegar
1 tbsp chopped fresh parsley
Salt and freshly ground black pepper

Hake with Pancetta Potatoes

Ingredients
½ tsp easy garlic
1 tbsp chopped fresh parsley
1 tbsp sundried tomato
   purée
1 tbsp grated Parmesan
   cheese
1 tbsp breadcrumbs
1 tbsp olive oil
Salt and freshly ground black
   pepper
120g hake fillet
1 tsp butter

For the potatoes
2 potatoes, peeled and diced
1 tbsp olive oil
2 shallots, chopped
2 slices of pancetta,
   chopped
2 plum tomatoes, halved

To serve
A green vegetable

This is moister than a crumble topping but the same idea, so don't be afraid to try it with different herbs, add some oats, or generally be free with your experimentation. Most kinds of fish would work cooked in this way. Try it in the halogen, too.

- Heat the oven to 180°C/Gas 4.

- Mix the garlic, parsley, tomato purée, Parmesan, breadcrumbs and about 1 tbsp olive oil to a paste in a mortar and pestle. Season with salt and pepper.

- Place the fish in a small ovenproof dish, cover with the mixture and dot with the butter. Bake in the oven for about 20 minutes until the fish is cooked and the topping crisp.

- Meanwhile, put the potatoes in a pan of water, bring to the boil, then simmer for about 3 minutes until almost tender.

- Heat the oil and fry the shallots for 3 minutes until soft but not browned.

- Add the pancetta and stir well together. Add the potatoes and continue to fry for 5–10 minutes until the potatoes are golden. Add the tomatoes and fry for 2 minutes.

- Serve the hake with the potatoes and a green vegetable.

Using the remaining pancetta
- Chop, fry and toss into pasta, use for Pasta Carbonara (page 129) or a Chicken Parcel (page 112).

Smoked Mackerel Risotto

This is a creamy and flavoursome risotto, infinitely variable by using different fish, prawns and scallops, chicken or vegetables. Here's a two-portion quantity so you can make Arancini (page 62) the next day but you can easily make it for one.

- Heat the oil and fry the shallots, garlic, celery and carrot for 5 minutes until soft.

- Stir in the thyme. Add the wine and stir until it has evaporated.

- Stir in the rice and stir the ingredients in the pan together until well mixed and the rice is shiny and hot.

- Gradually add the hot stock a spoonful at a time, keeping the ingredients at a gentle simmer and stirring each addition until it has all been absorbed. Add the milk between each addition. It will take about 20 minutes.

- Stir in the smoked mackerel with the last addition of stock so that it heats through. Taste and season with a little salt, if needed, and plenty of pepper.

- Remove from the heat and stir in the crème fraîche, cover and leave to rest for 5 minutes before serving half and saving half to make Arancini.

Using the remaining celery and smoked mackerel
- Use the rest of the celery in the base for other recipes, in salads (page 138), for soup (page 32) or as a vegetable.

- Fold some flaked smoked mackerel through couscous and serve with crusty bread and salad or use the fish for Smoked Mackerel and Potato Salad (page 63).

Ingredients
1 tbsp olive oil
2 shallots, chopped
1 small garlic clove, chopped
1 small celery stick, chopped
1 small carrot, chopped
1 tsp chopped fresh thyme
2 tbsp dry white wine
200g Arborio or other risotto rice
600ml hot fish or vegetable stock
100ml milk
4 smoked mackerel fillets, skinned and flaked
Salt and freshly ground black pepper
2 tbsp crème fraîche

Arancini

Ingredients
½ quantity Smoked
  Mackerel Risotto (page
  61) or other risotto
2 tbsp plain flour
1 egg, beaten
100g fine breadcrumbs
Olive oil for frying

I first enjoyed Arancini on holiday in Sicily, strolling along in the Mediterranean sunshine. A kind of southern Italian bubble and squeak, in a way, as it uses leftover risotto, which is coated in breadcrumbs and fried.

- Roll the risotto into small balls – traditionally they are bigger than tennis balls but I make them more like golf balls.

- Roll in the plain flour to coat, then in the beaten egg, then in the fine breadcrumbs.

- Heat the oil and shallow-fry, turning frequently, for about 5 minutes until golden brown and piping hot right through.

- Serve hot or cold.

Smoked Mackerel and Potato Salad

This makes for quite a substantial salad using the smallest waxy potatoes you can find, or you could dice larger potatoes. The cornichon will add a little sharpness to the salad, but I wouldn't buy them just for this recipe.

- Put the potatoes and mint in a pan, cover with salted water and bring to the boil. Simmer for about 10 minutes until cooked.

- Meanwhile, beat the egg yolk, lemon juice, garlic and mustard with a twist of salt. Gradually pour in the oil, whisking all the time, until the mixture thickens.

- Stir in the capers, spring onions, mint and cornichon, if using. Season to taste with salt and pepper.

- Drain the potatoes well, discarding the mint sprig, and halve or quarter, if necessary. Stir enough of the dressing into the potatoes to coat them; you may have a little left over for tomorrow's salad.

- Pile the salad leaves on a plate, top with the potato salad and arrange the mackerel on top to serve.

Using the remaining smoked mackerel
- Fold some flaked smoked mackerel through couscous and serve with crusty bread and salad or use the fish for Smoked Mackerel Risotto (page 61).

Ingredients
150g baby salad potatoes
Sprig of mint
Salt and freshly ground
   black pepper
1 egg yolk
½ tsp lemon juice
¼ tsp easy garlic
¼ tsp Dijon mustard
150ml oil
1 tsp capers, chopped
2–3 spring onions, finely
   chopped
A few mint leaves, chopped
1 cornichon, chopped
   (optional)
Handful of fresh salad
   leaves
1–2 smoked mackerel
   fillets, skinned and
   flaked

Beef

When you are cooking beef, it is very much a case of making sure you have the right cut for the right job. To cook quickly, you must use a quality steak or it will just be tough and tasteless; that means it will be more expensive. Choose a thick steak marbled with fat and leave it in the fridge, uncovered, for a day before cooking in a very hot pan, turning frequently until browned on the outside but succulent on the inside.

Cheaper cuts, on the other hand, respond to long, slow cooking and, if you do that, you can't go far wrong. The disadvantage for the single cook is that it's a bit of a waste having the oven on for hours just for one meal, so many of the recipes in this chapter are designed in larger quantities so you can cook efficiently and economically, then freeze portions to serve another day.

Home-made Burger with Caramelised Onion Chutney

Ingredients
500g minced beef
50g breadcrumbs
1 onion, finely chopped
2 garlic cloves, chopped
2 tbsp chopped fresh parsley
1 tbsp tomato purée
Pinch of paprika
Salt and freshly ground black
  pepper
1 egg
2 tbsp plain flour
1 tbsp olive oil

To serve per person
1 burger bun
Handful of salad leaves
1 tsp mayonnaise
Squirt of Dijon mustard
1 slice of Gouda cheese
Sauté Chips (page 47) or use
  oven chips
Caramelised onion chutney

If you make your own burgers, you know exactly what is in them, can flavour them to suit your own taste, and then wrap and freeze them individually so you can take them out and cook whenever you like.

- Put all the burger ingredients, except the egg, flour and oil, into a food processor and process until well blended. You can leave the mixture fairly chunky or make it smoother. Add the egg and process again.

- Shape the mixture into 8 burgers, pressing together firmly using floured hands to stop the mixture sticking.

- Wrap 6 of the burgers in clingfilm, label and freeze.

- Heat the oil and fry, griddle or grill the burgers for about 5 minutes on each side until cooked through and browned.

- Assemble your burger in the bun with the salad, mayonnaise, mustard and cheese, or condiments of your choice, and serve with chips and caramelised onion chutney.

Serving the remaining portions
- Serve the remaining burgers in the same way; with different breads; without bread or buns; with melted cheese on top, perhaps a blue cheese for a change.

Spaghetti and Meatballs with Tomato Sauce

It's unlikely you'd bother to make meatballs for one, but if you make enough for four, then freeze the ones you are not going to cook immediately, you've saved yourself a job for another day. You could make them larger if you prefer.

- To make the meatballs, put all the ingredients except the egg in a food processor, seasoning with a little salt and plenty of pepper, and process until finely chopped. Add the egg and process until blended.

- Remove from the bowl and, with floured hands, shape the mixture into small balls. Wrap, label and freeze what you don't need.

- Heat the oil and fry the meatballs gently for about 15 minutes, turning frequently until browned and cooked through.

- Meanwhile, bring a pan of salted water to the boil, add the spaghetti, return to the boil and cook for about 5 minutes until *al dente*.

- In another pan, heat the tomato sauce.

- Drain the cooked pasta, add to the tomato sauce and stir to coat, then stir in the meatballs and serve sprinkled with more pepper and plenty of Parmesan.

Ingredients

For the meatballs
500g minced beef
1 bacon rasher, chopped
1 onion, chopped
2 slices of bread, roughly torn into pieces
1 tsp dried oregano
25g Parmesan cheese, finely grated
Salt and freshly ground black pepper
1 egg

To finish
2 tbsp plain flour
2 tbsp olive oil
100–150g spaghetti
300ml Tomato Sauce (page 136)
A few Parmesan shavings

Tagliatelle Bolognese

Ingredients

3 tbsp olive oil
2 onions, chopped
2 carrots, chopped
2 celery sticks, chopped
1–2 garlic cloves, chopped
500g minced beef
150ml red wine
2 tbsp sun-dried tomato
  purée
2 x 400g cans of chopped
  tomatoes
1 tbsp dried oregano
Salt and freshly ground black
  pepper
A few fresh basil leaves

To serve
100g tagliatelle

In Italy, this dish is reserved for special occasions because it should be cooked for several hours. This is a cook-in recipe for a large quantity, then you can serve the remaining portions in the same way or in different variations.

- Heat the oil and fry the onions, carrots, celery and garlic for 5 minutes until soft but not browned.

- Add the meat and stir in until well mixed, browned and the grains are separate.

- Add the wine and stir for 5 minutes to boil off the alcohol.

- Stir in the tomato purée, tomatoes and oregano, then season with salt and pepper.

- Bring to the boil, then simmer gently for 1½–2 hours, stirring occasionally, until the sauce is thick, checking occasionally and tasting and adjusting the seasoning towards the end of the cooking time.

- Serve one portion garnished with basil leaves.

- Cool, wrap, label and freeze the remaining portions.

- **Lasagne:** Make 150ml of White Sauce by whisking 1 tbsp of flour and 1 tbsp butter into 120ml milk and simmering for 3 minutes, and flavour it with a little grated Parmesan. Rinse 2 or 3 sheets of lasagne pasta in boiling water. Assemble a lasagne in a small dish, layering meat, pasta and sauce and finishing with a layer of sauce sprinkled with Parmesan. Bake in a hot oven at 200°C/Gas 6 for about 20 minutes until heated through and golden and bubbling on top.

- **Cannelloni with Blue Cheese:** Rinse some cannelloni tubes in boiling water, then stuff with a portion of the mixture. Arrange in a shallow ovenproof dish and cover generously with grated or crumbled blue cheese, or a cheese of your choice. Bake in a hot oven at 200°C/Gas 6 for about 20 minutes until heated through and golden and bubbling on top.

- **Minced Beef Pie:** Heat the oven to 200°C/Gas 6 and place a baking sheet in the oven. Roll out a puff pastry portion and cut in half. Use half to line a greased pie tin, then fill with the mixture and moisten the edges. Roll out the remaining pastry into a circle and seal on the top, crimping the edges together and trimming them. Make leaves or patterns on the top with the remaining pastry, if you wish, brushing with beaten egg to make them stick and to glaze the top of the pie. Place the pie dish on the hot baking sheet and bake in the oven for about 20 minutes until heated through and golden.

Baked Stuffed Mushrooms

Ingredients
1 large mushroom
1 tsp olive oil
100g minced beef
1 shallot, finely chopped
½ tsp easy garlic
2 tbsp cooked long-grain
   rice
1 tbsp Tomato Sauce (page
   136), tomato ketchup or
   passata
Dash of Worcestershire sauce
1 tsp chopped fresh parsley
Salt and freshly ground black
   pepper
2 tbsp stock
1 tbsp breadcrumbs
2 tbsp grated cheese

To serve
Salad

You can make this with a beefsteak tomato if you prefer, hollowing it out, then mixing the flesh with the stuffing. If you like, you can use one portion of your Bolognese (page 68) mixture as the stuffing, or use cooked meat and omit the frying.

- Heat the oven to 190°C/Gas 5.

- Remove the stalk from the mushroom and chop it. Place the mushroom in an ovenproof dish, gill-side up.

- Heat the oil and fry the beef, shallot and garlic until the meat is browned. Remove from the heat.

- Stir in the chopped mushroom, then the rice, tomato sauce, Worcestershire sauce and parsley, and season with salt and pepper.

- Spoon the stock over the mushroom, then pile the mixture into the mushroom, pressing it down lightly. Sprinkle with the breadcrumbs and cheese.

- Bake in the oven for about 15 minutes until cooked through and golden on top.

- Serve with salad.

Cook's tip
- This works well in the halogen.

Beef, Bacon and Egg

If you don't have any leftover beef to use for this recipe, just use some cooked beef from a packet, or try it with other cooked meats. You can use beef, lamb, pork or chicken to make a surprisingly tasty dish that is quick and easy to make.

- Heat the butter and oil and fry the bacon and shallot for 2 minutes.

- Add the potato and fry for a few minutes over a high heat until golden. Drain off any excess oil.

- Add the meat, parsley, Worcestershire sauce, salt and pepper and cook, stirring gently, for 5–10 minutes until hot.

- Meanwhile, fry the egg until cooked to your liking.

- Spoon the meat onto your plate and top with the egg to serve.

Ingredients
½ tbsp butter
½ tsp olive oil
2 bacon rashers, diced
1 shallot, chopped
1 cooked potato, diced
100g cooked beef, diced
2 tsp chopped fresh parsley
Dash of Worcestershire
   sauce
Salt and freshly ground
   black pepper
1 egg

Beef in Red Wine

Ingredients

900g braising steak, diced
4 rashers of bacon, chopped
300ml red wine
2 tbsp olive oil
3 onions, thinly sliced
2 tbsp plain flour
2 tbsp butter
4 carrots, thickly sliced
2 parsnips, thickly sliced
2 garlic cloves, chopped
1 sprig of fresh rosemary
1 bouquet garni
500ml beef stock
3 tbsp tomato purée
3 tbsp redcurrant jelly
Salt and freshly ground black
    pepper
1 tbsp chopped fresh parsley

To serve
Mashed garlic potatoes

I think a slow-cooked casserole always benefits from a dash of wine. This is definitely a dish to leave cooking for a long time so make it one of your 'cook-in' dishes and freeze it in portions to enjoy more than once.

- Put the beef and bacon in a bowl, pour over the wine, cover and leave to marinate overnight.

- Lift the meat and bacon into a colander to drain, reserving the marinade.

- Heat the oven to 160°C/Gas 3.

- Heat the oil and fry the onions for about 5 minutes until soft.

- Toss the beef and bacon in the flour to coat, then add to the pan and fry over a high heat for about 5 minutes until just browned. Transfer to a casserole dish using a slotted spoon.

- Reduce the heat to medium, add the butter to the pan and fry the carrots, parsnips and garlic for 5 minutes, then transfer to the casserole dish and add the rosemary and the bouquet garni.

- Pour the stock into the pan, add the tomato purée and redcurrant jelly and bring to the boil, scraping up all the cooking juices. Pour over the ingredients in the casserole and season with salt and pepper.

- Cover and cook in the oven for about 3 hours until the meat is tender and the sauce thick, stirring occasionally.

- To make the mashed potatoes, simply boil and mash potatoes as usual, with a knob of butter, a dash of milk and ½ tsp easy garlic per serving.

- Discard the bouquet garni before serving the casserole with the mashed potatoes.

Serving the remaining portions

- **Beef Cobbler:** Put the casserole in an individual dish. Make a cobbler topping by rubbing 1 tbsp butter and 1 tbsp lard into 4 tbsp self-raising flour (or plain with a pinch of baking powder), then working to a dough with about 1 tbsp water. Roll out to the size of the casserole, mark into segments, pop on the top of the meat and brush with a little milk. Reheat in the oven at 190°C/Gas 5 for about 25 minutes until the meat is hot and the cobbler is cooked and golden.

- **Beef in Baked Potatoes:** Cook a baking potato in the microwave for 4 minutes to soften, then put it in the oven at 200°C/Gas 6. Put the casserole portion in an ovenproof dish, stir in an extra 1 tbsp redcurrant jelly, cover and put in the oven. Cook for about 25 minutes until the casserole is piping hot and the potato soft inside with a crisp skin. Cut the potato in a star shape and push it open, then spoon the casserole over and top with a spoonful of crème fraîche.

- **Beef and Wine Pie:** Put a portion of casserole in an ovenproof dish. Roll out a portion of puff pastry. Use a brush dipped in milk or water to moisten the edge of the dish, then place the pastry on top, folding it carefully over the sides. Bake in the oven at 200°C/Gas 6 for about 20 minutes until heated through and the top is golden and crisp.

Minced Beef with Chilli and Kidney Beans

Ingredients
2 tbsp olive oil
1 onion, chopped
1 garlic clove, chopped
1 red chilli, seeded and
    chopped
1 tsp paprika
1 carrot, finely chopped
500g minced beef
2 tbsp sundried tomato
    purée
300ml beef stock
400g can of passata
400g can of red kidney
    beans, rinsed and drained
Salt and freshly ground black
    pepper
1 tbsp chopped fresh parsley

To serve
Boiled rice

Rub a little olive oil over your hands before you handle chillis and avoid touching your face, especially your eyes or mouth, with chilli oil on your hands. Adjust the spiciness to suit your own taste.

- Heat the oil and fry the onion, garlic, chilli, paprika and carrot for 5 minutes until soft.

- Add the mince and fry for a few minutes until browned and the grains are separate, stirring well.

- Stir in the tomato purée, then the stock and passata, bring to the boil, then simmer for about 1 hour until the sauce is thick.

- Add the beans and season with salt and pepper. Continue to cook for about 10 minutes until the beans are hot and the whole dish is well blended.

- Sprinkle with parsley and serve with rice.

Serving the remaining portions

- **Spiced Beef Wraps:** Reheat the mince in a pan with 2 tbsp extra stock or water to moisten. Warm 2 flour tortillas and prepare a handful of grated carrot, raw beetroot or salad leaves. Wrap the beef in the tortillas with some of your chosen salad and a dollop of guacamole, soured cream or mayonnaise.

- **Spicy Mince with Sweet Potato:** Peel, boil and mash a sweet potato. Put a portion of the spiced beef in an ovenproof dish, top with the mash and dot with butter. Heat through in the oven at 200°C/Gas 6 for about 25 minutes, or about 20 in a halogen.

- **Filo Beef Parcels:** Make your parcels as large or small as you like. Brush a few strips of filo pastry with oil, put a spoonful of mince on the corner and fold over the corner to create a triangle. Continue to fold to encase the filling. Brush with oil and bake in the oven at 200°C/Gas 6 for about 15 minutes until golden.

Steak with Gorgonzola Mash

Choose a thick steak, well marbled with fat, for the best results. Unwrap it and leave it in the fridge for a day to mature. Bring it to room temperature before you cook it.

- Put the potato in a pan, cover with salted water, bring to the boil, then simmer for about 10 minutes until tender.

- Meanwhile, heat the oil until very hot and fry the steak quickly for about 2 minutes each side, turning frequently, so that it is just seared on both sides. Leave in the pan to rest for 5 minutes while you finish the potatoes and make the salad.

- Drain, then mash the potatoes with the butter and a little of the cheese, then fold in the remaining cheese. Season with pepper; it should not need any more salt.

- Mix the rocket and walnuts. Whisk together the honey, lemon juice, olive oil and mustard and drizzle over the salad.

- Place the steak on top and spoon the potato on the side to serve.

Ingredients
1 large potato, peeled and diced
Salt and freshly ground black pepper
1 tbsp olive oil
1 small sirloin steak, at room temperature
1 tbsp butter
50g Gorgonzola or other blue cheese, crumbled

For the salad
2 handfuls of rocket
2 tbsp walnut halves
1 tsp honey
2 tsp lemon juice
2 tbsp olive oil
A little Dijon mustard

Lamb

Lamb is a wonderful meat but it can be expensive, so when you do cook lamb, don't waste anything. It is quite delicate so cook it gently so that it is seared on the outside but remains pink and succulent in the middle.

Spring is the traditional time for lamb so serve it with locally grown fresh spring vegetables. Chops, cutlets and other cuts are all designed perfectly for those cooking just to please themselves.

Lamb with Minted Mash

Ingredients

2 tbsp plain flour
Salt and freshly ground black
  pepper
600g neck of lamb, cut into
  chunks
2 rashers lean bacon,
  chopped
2 tbsp oil
1 onion, chopped
2 carrots, chopped
1 celery stick, chopped
100g mushrooms, quartered
  or sliced
300ml red wine
300ml meat or vegetable
  stock
2 bay leaves
Small bunch of fresh thyme
Dash of Worcestershire sauce
2 potatoes, peeled and diced
1 tbsp butter
A little milk
1 tsp mint jelly

To serve

Green vegetables

The recipe works with pork, too, although lamb with mint is the traditional combination. Try other fresh herbs in your mashed potatoes, or stir in a spoonful of easy garlic.

- Heat the oven to 180°C/Gas 4.

- Season the flour with salt and pepper, then toss the lamb and bacon in the flour to coat, shaking off any excess.

- Heat 1 tbsp of the oil in a frying pan and fry the meat for a few minutes until browned, then transfer to a casserole dish.

- Add the remaining oil to the frying pan and fry the onion, carrots and celery for about 5 minutes until just soft.

- Add the mushrooms and fry for 2 minutes, then spoon the vegetables into the casserole.

- Pour the wine and stock into the pan with the herbs and Worcestershire sauce and bring to the boil, scraping up any residue. Pour into the casserole and season with salt and pepper.

- Cover and cook in the oven for 1½ hours.

- Meanwhile, cook the potatoes in boiling salted water for about 10 minutes until tender. Drain, then mash with the butter and milk, then stir in the mint jelly to taste.

- Serve one portion of the casserole with the minted mash and some green vegetables.

- Cool, wrap, label and freeze the remaining portions.

Serving the remaining portions

- **Lamb Cobbler:** A cobbler is basically a casserole with savoury scones on the top, doing away with the need for an accompaniment – although a sprinkling of mint sauce doesn't go amiss. To make, rub 20g lard and 20g butter into 100g plain flour, ½ tsp baking powder and ½ tsp chopped fresh thyme until the mixture resembles breadcrumbs. Gradually pour in 1–2 tbsp water to make the mixture bind together. Roll it out to 4cm thick on a lightly floured surface and cut into rounds with a cookie cutter. Heat the casserole in a pan, then transfer to an ovenproof dish. Arrange the scones on top of the casserole, brush with a little milk and cook in a preheated oven at 200°C/Gas 6 for about 10 minutes until the cobbler is cooked and golden.

- **Lamb with Green Lentils:** Put a portion of the casserole in a pan and add 300ml water and 2 tbsp green lentils. Bring to the boil, stirring, then simmer for about 20 minutes until the lentils are tender.

- **Lamb Cheat Cassoulet:** Stir a drained can of haricot beans, or other beans or pulses, and some chunks of cooked sausage into the portion in an overproof dish. Reheat in a preheated oven at 200°C/Gas 6 for about 10 minutes until the casserole is thoroughly heated, stirring occasionally.

Stuffed Minted Aubergine

Ingredients
1 medium aubergine
2 tbsp olive oil
Salt and freshly ground black pepper
6 tbsp hot stock
1 tbsp lemon juice
50g couscous, toasted
120g minced lamb
½ tsp easy garlic
1 tbsp chopped fresh mint
1 tbsp tomato purée
Dash of harissa
Pinch of ground cinnamon
2 baby plum tomatoes, coarsely chopped
2 tsp chopped fresh parsley

To serve
Green salad

Aubergines vary considerably in size, so choose one that matches your appetite, or go for the tiny aubergines – a bit more fiddly. Lamb mince is usually sold in 250g packs so use half and freeze half.

- Heat the oven to 180°C/Gas 4.

- Halve the aubergine lengthways, drizzle with a little of the oil and cook in the oven for 10 minutes until tender.

- Pour the hot stock and lemon juice over the couscous, stir and leave to stand.

- Meanwhile heat half the remaining oil and fry the lamb and garlic for 10 minutes until browned.

- Remove the aubergine from the oven, scoop out the inside and chop.

- Stir the mint, tomato purée, harissa and cinnamon into the meat, then remove from the heat and gently stir in the aubergine, tomatoes and couscous. Season with salt and pepper.

- Pile the mixture back into and around the aubergine shells and return to the oven for 10 minutes until crisp on top.

- Garnish with the parsley and serve with a green salad.

Lamb Cutlets with Sweet Spinach

Lamb cutlets or chops are quite small so you will probably need two. Toast pine nuts in a dry pan, shaking it over a medium heat for a few minutes until golden; this will give them a nuttier flavour.

- Brush the cutlets with half the oil and season with salt and pepper. Place under a hot grill for about 15 minutes until cooked on both sides but still slightly pink in the middle.

- Meanwhile, crush the garlic and anchovy fillet into the remaining oil and season with salt and pepper. Place in a pan over a medium heat to heat through.

- Add the raisins and pine nuts.

- Rinse and shake the spinach, then add to the pan with just the water remaining on the leaves. Toss in the oil and stir over a moderate heat for a few minutes until it is beginning to wilt. Season with salt and pepper.

- Grate a little nutmeg over the spinach and serve with the cutlets and some mashed or crushed new potatoes.

Using the remaining pine nuts
- These appear in a number of recipes, including Minted Chicken Salad (page 114), but you can add them to any salad or sprinkle them on cooked vegetables or beans.

Ingredients
2 lamb cutlets
1 tbsp oil
Salt and freshly ground
    black pepper
½ tsp easy garlic
1 anchovy fillet
2 tbsp raisins
2 tbsp toasted pine nuts
150g spinach
Sprinkling of grated
    nutmeg

To serve
Crushed new potatoes

Lamb Chops with Shallots and Peas

Ingredients
2 tsp olive oil
2 lamb chops
2 shallots, quartered
1 tbsp caster sugar
100g frozen peas
Handful of fresh mint,
    roughly chopped
Squeeze of lemon juice
Salt and freshly ground black
    pepper

To serve
New potatoes
Sprig of fresh mint

Cook this dish in one pan to save on energy and washing up. Mint is the perfect companion for lamb. You can add some mint sauce or mint jelly on the side if you like. If you buy mint jelly, snip in a few extra fresh mint leaves.

- Heat the oil and put the chops at the side of the pan.

- Add the shallots and fry until just beginning to brown, then reduce the heat, add the sugar and cook for about 10 minutes until soft. The chops can continue to cook at the side of the pan, turning occasionally.

- Meanwhile, cook the peas in boiling water for about 2 minutes until tender, then drain well.

- Stir the peas into the shallots with the mint and lemon juice, and season to taste with salt and pepper.

- Serve with boiled new potatoes and garnish with the fresh mint.

Lamb Shank with Rosemary and Garlic

A lamb shank is a substantial piece of meat, and although it is probably more than one everyday portion, this recipe is perfect either for treating yourself, for serving for two, or for copying using a leg or other joint.

- Heat the oven to 200°C/Gas 6.

- Cut one of the garlic cloves into slivers and chop the second. Pierce slits in the meat with the tip of a sharp knife and press slivers of anchovy and garlic into the meat. Season with salt and pepper.

- Heat the oil on a fairly high heat and fry the shank for about 5 minutes until browned all over. Place in an ovenproof dish.

- Reduce the heat to medium, add the shallots to the pan and fry for a few minutes until soft. Add to the casserole.

- Pour the wine, stock and tomatoes into the pan, bring to the boil, then pour over the meat. Add the rosemary and cover the dish.

- Reduce the oven temperature to 160°C/Gas 3 and cook in the oven for about 3 hours, turning and basting occasionally, until the lamb is so tender it falls off the bone.

- If the sauce is too thin, remove the lid and increase the oven temperature for 10–15 minutes.

- Garnish with parsley and serve with mashed potatoes and a green vegetable.

Ingredients
2 garlic cloves
1 lamb shank
2 anchovy fillets, cut into slivers
Salt and freshly ground black pepper
1 tbsp olive oil
3 shallots, thickly sliced
150ml red wine
150ml lamb or chicken stock
1 x 200g can of chopped tomatoes
1 sprig of fresh rosemary
1 tbsp chopped fresh parsley

To serve
Mashed potatoes
Green vegetable

Braised Tender Lamb

Ingredients
2 tbsp olive oil
1 onion, sliced
500g diced lamb
1 garlic clove, chopped
1 red pepper, diced
1 tbsp sundried tomato
    purée
400g can of tomatoes
300ml chicken stock
1 tsp dried basil
Salt and freshly ground black
    pepper

To serve
Baked potato
Fresh vegetables

Shoulder is a good cut for slow cooking, so buy it whole and dice it, or buy ready-prepared meat to make this 'cook-in' dish. Reheat single portions in the preheated halogen for about 5 minutes.

- Heat the oven to 160°C/Gas 3.

- Heat the oil and fry the onion for 5 minutes.

- Add the lamb, garlic and pepper and stir for about 5 minutes until browned.

- Stir in the tomato purée and tomatoes, stock and basil, and season to taste with salt and pepper.

- Transfer to an ovenproof dish, cover and cook in the oven for about 2 hours until the meat is tender. Put a potato in the oven after an hour so it is ready at the same time.

- Serve one portion with the potato and fresh vegetables.

- Wrap, label and freeze the remaining portions.

Serving the remaining portions
- **Lamb with Mediterranean Couscous:** Make some couscous (see page 52) to go with the reheated lamb.

- **Lamb with Crisp Courgettes:** Shave slices off a courgette with a potato peeler and grill them or cook them in a griddle pan so they are nicely marked. Reheat the lamb with a generous spoonful of redcurrant jelly, stirring it well into the juices.

- **Lamb with Parsnip Topping:** Peel and slice a parsnip and boil in salted water for 5 minutes until soft. Drain well. Spoon the casserole into an ovenproof dish, arrange the parsnips on top and brush with butter. Reheat in the oven at 200°C/Gas 6 for about 15 minutes until piping hot and crisp on top.

• Lamb

Lamb Steaks with Mustard and Redcurrant

Redcurrant jelly gives a richness of flavour to a lamb sauce that I love. I have two friends with allotments who always give me a pot of their home-made redcurrant jelly at Christmas – delicious!

- Mix the soured cream with the garlic and mustard and season with salt and pepper. Rub into the chops and leave to stand for an hour, if possible.

- Heat the oil and fry the chops to seal on both sides, then add the wine and redcurrant jelly and cook, whisking occasionally, for about 10 minutes until the meat is tender.

- Serve with mashed potatoes and peas or broccoli.

Cook's tip
- Instead of soured cream, just use cream with a dash of lemon juice. This recipe works with pork escalopes too.

Ingredients
2 tbsp soured cream
½ tsp easy garlic
½ tsp Dijon mustard
Salt and freshly ground
    black pepper
2 lamb loin chops
2 tsp olive oil
2 tbsp red wine
2 tbsp redcurrant jelly

To serve
Mashed potatoes
Peas or broccoli

Pork

Pork makes for some delicious recipes but does need a little care in the cooking otherwise it can go a bit tough and stringy. If in doubt, longer, slower cooking times tend to give me the best results.

If you buy pork with a fatty rind, you can cut that off before you cook the meat, or cook it on a rack so that the fat drains away.

Pork complements so many flavours of herbs and accompaniments, and is particularly good with fruity flavours, hence the old favourite of serving pork with apple sauce.

Pork with Lemon Pasta

Ingredients
2 tsp olive oil
1 pork steak, cut into strips
2 shallots, chopped
½ tsp easy garlic
1 tsp Dijon mustard
2 tsp lemon juice
About 6 tbsp milk
Salt and freshly ground black
    pepper
100g pasta
3 tbsp crème fraîche
2 tbsp grated Parmesan

To serve
Mixed salad

This makes a lovely light sauce to coat the pork and pasta. You can use cream intead of crème fraîche if you prefer or even a mild cream cheese. Don't allow a sauce to boil once you have added crème fraîche or it will curdle.

- Heat the oil and fry the steak strips over a high heat for a couple of minutes, then reduce the heat to medium, add the shallots and fry for 5 minutes. Stir in the garlic and fry for 2 minutes. Stir in the mustard, lemon juice and milk, and season with salt and pepper.

- Meanwhile, cook the pasta in boiling salted water for about 8 minutes until *al dente*. Drain well.

- Reduce the heat under the pork to a minimum, then stir in the crème fraîche. Do not allow the mixture to boil.

- Gently toss the meat with the pasta, sprinkle with Parmesan and serve with salad.

Makes 1 serving

Pork Rolls with Gorgonzola

If you don't have a rolling pin, use a clean milk bottle or a meat mallet to pound the escalope so it is thin; this also tenderises the meat. You could use other cheeses if you like but choose something with plenty of flavour.

- Flatten the pork with a rolling pin, top with the cheese and sage leaves, then roll up tightly and secure with cocktail sticks. Season with salt and pepper.

- Roll in the flour, then the egg, then the breadcrumbs.

- Heat the oil and fry the pork roll for about 10 minutes on all sides, turning frequently, until golden. Reduce the heat slightly and continue to cook for a further 5–10 minutes until the meat is tender.

- Lift the pork from the pan and keep it warm.

- Pour the wine and stock into the pan and bring to the boil, then spoon over the pork.

- Serve with celeriac mash and green beans.

Ingredients
1 pork escalope or loin steak
1 thick slice Gorgonzola cheese
2 sage leaves
Salt and freshly ground black pepper
1 tbsp plain flour
1 egg, beaten
50g breadcrumbs
1 tbsp olive oil
2 tbsp red wine
2 tbsp chicken stock

To serve
Celeriac mash
Green beans

Pork Tortilla Wraps

Ingredients
125g pork fillet, thinly sliced
½ tsp fajita seasoning
2–3 mushrooms, sliced
1 small carrot, grated
½ courgette, grated
¼ red pepper, diced
2–3 flour tortilla wraps

For the salsa
2 baby plum tomatoes,
    quartered
50g canned sweetcorn,
    drained
¼ red pepper, finely
    chopped
¼ courgette, finely chopped
2 tsp chopped fresh
    coriander
1 tbsp lime or lemon juice
2 tsp olive oil

A whole pork fillet, or tenderloin, will make about four servings, so you can either cook it all, or cut it into four before you freeze three portions and cook one. It is a very lean piece of meat and perfect for pan-fried dishes.

- Dry-fry the pork slices in a hot non-stick wok for 5 minutes.

- Add the fajita seasoning, mushrooms, carrot, courgette and pepper, and cook for a further 1–2 minutes, adding a little boiling water if the mixture is too dry.

- Meanwhile, mix together the salsa ingredients.

- Warm the tortilla wraps. Pile the meat into the tortillas and wrap them up, then serve with the tomato salsa.

Using the remaining sweetcorn
- Use as a vegetable, for Sweetcorn Pancakes (page 133) or Chicken and Sweetcorn Chowder (page 27).

Pork Escalope with Rhubarb

Individual cuts, such as chops, are made for singles! Quite often, though, they come in packs of two, so split them and freeze one for another day. This was meant to be made with apples but I had forgotten to buy them – the result was more interesting.

- Toss the rhubarb in the lemon juice. Season the chop with salt and pepper.

- Heat the oil and fry the pork on both sides for about 8 minutes until golden and crisp.

- Add the shallot and fry for 3 minutes.

- Add the rhubarb and turn in the juices, then stir in the orange juice and season with salt and pepper. Simmer gently for about 10 minutes until the chop is cooked.

- Serve with garlic mash and peas.

Cook's tip
- You can also make this with apple and apple juice.

Ingredients
2 sticks of rhubarb, chopped
1 tsp lemon juice
1 pork chop or pork escalope
Salt and freshly ground black pepper
1 tsp olive oil
1 shallot, chopped
100ml orange juice

To serve
Garlic mashed potatoes
Peas

Roast Pork with Gravy

Ingredients
1 shoulder of pork
2 tbsp olive oil
Salt and freshly ground black
   pepper
1 tbsp cornflour
600ml chicken stock

To serve
Mashed potatoes
Carrots
Pease pudding
Apple sauce

If you are going to roast pork, then you need a big piece so that it stays moist and juicy. Shoulder of pork is economical. Give it a long slow cook in the oven for succulent results.

- Heat the oven to 220°C/Gas 7.

- Rub the pork skin with oil and season with salt. Place in a baking tin and roast in the oven for 20 minutes until the crackling is crunchy.

- Reduce the oven temperature to 160°C/Gas 3 and roast for 5 hours.

- Lift out the meat, cover with foil and leave to rest for 5 minutes.

- Lift off the crackling and cut into chunks. Shred the meat with two forks.

- Whisk the cornflour into the meat juices, then whisk in the stock and bring to the boil on the hob, scraping up all the juices into the gravy.

- Serve the pork, gravy and crackling with mashed potatoes, carrots, pease pudding and apple sauce.

- Cool, wrap, label and freeze the remaining portions.

Variation
Everyone has a different idea about how to create the crunchiest crackling. If you don't find this technique successful, try leaving the meat uncovered in the fridge overnight before you cook it. Then either cook as above or put it straight in the hot oven without the oil or salt.

Serving the remaining portions

- **Pork Wraps:** Reheat a portion of the pork. Warm some flour tortillas and wrap forkfuls of pork with some rocket, caramelised onion chutney and soured cream.

- **Oriental Honeyed Pork:** Whisk together 1 tbsp honey, 1 tsp wine vinegar, 1 tbsp tomato purée and 1 tsp Dijon mustard and season with salt and pepper. Reheat a portion of pork in a pan, then toss in the mixture and turn the meat until heated through and well coated. Meanwhile, drop ½ block of egg noodles into a pan of boiling water or stock and boil for 2 minutes until just soft, then drain. Add to the meat and stir together. Serve garnished with chopped spring onion.

- **Pork Fries:** Mix some shredded pork with mashed potato and a chopped spring onion, a sprinkling of chopped herbs, salt and pepper and an egg. Roll into balls and fry for 8 minutes until crisp on all sides.

Soy Pork Noodles

Ingredients
1 tbsp olive oil
1 stick lemongrass, chopped,
   or ½ tsp easy lemongrass
½ tsp easy ginger
½ red pepper, chopped
2 spring onions, chopped
1 tbsp plain flour
Salt and freshly ground black
   pepper
100g pork pieces
½ block egg noodles
1 tbsp soy sauce

You can now buy easy lemongrass in small jars so although it's not as good as the real thing, it's useful to have in the cupboard if you like to surprise yourself and rustle up something Asian-style now and again.

- Heat the oil and fry the lemongrass, ginger, pepper and spring onions for 2 minutes.

- Season the flour with salt and pepper, then toss the pork in the flour, shaking off the excess. Add to the pan and fry, stirring, for a few minutes until browned on all sides.

- Meanwhile, bring a large pan of salted water to the boil, add the noodles, and boil for 2 minutes, or as directed on the packet.

- Add the soy sauce to the meat and toss everything together for 3–5 minutes until the meat is cooked.

- Drain the noodles well, then add to the pan, toss together and serve.

Makes 4 servings

Minced Pork Meatloaf

This meatloaf is so easy to make and you can serve it hot or cold for supper, lunch or to add to a lunch box. You could use almost any mince but pork works particularly well. Vary the herbs to ring the changes.

- Heat the oven to 180°C/Gas 4 and line a 450g loaf tin with a loaf tin liner or baking parchment.

- Mix together all the ingredients except the chilli and milk. Add chilli to taste, if liked, and season to taste with salt and pepper. The mixture should be quite sticky and hold together. If it is too dry, add a little milk; if it is too wet, add some more breadcrumbs.

- Spoon into the prepared tin and press down gently.

- Bake in the oven for about 1 hour until firm to the touch and browned on the top.

- Turn out and slice one portion to serve hot topped with a fried egg and accompanied by mashed potatoes or chips and baked beans.

Serving the remaining portions
- Leave the meatloaf to cool, then wrap in clingfilm and keep in the fridge to serve sliced with crusty bread and pickles for lunch, or wrap, label and freeze to serve another time.

350g minced pork
2 tbsp fresh breadcrumbs
1 onion, finely chopped
½ tsp easy garlic
2 tbsp tomato purée
2 tbsp water
1 tbsp chopped fresh parsley
1 small egg, lightly beaten
Salt and freshly ground black pepper
A dash of chilli sauce (optional)
A little milk (optional)

To serve
Fried egg
Mashed potatoes or chips
Baked beans

Farm Sausages with Roasted Vegetables

Ingredients
2–3 good quality sausages
1 red onion, cut into chunks
1 red pepper, cut into
  chunks
1 garlic clove
1 tbsp olive oil (optional)
Salt and freshly ground black
  pepper
½ x 200g can of artichoke
  hearts, drained and halved
2 plum tomatoes

To serve
Mashed sweet potatoes
Chutney

If you buy high-quality farm or supermarket sausages, you'll get the best flavour. This makes a generous serving, but you can use any leftover vegetables as a side dish the next day. It cooks in the halogen in 15 minutes.

- Heat the oven to 200°C/Gas 6.

- Put the sausages in a small baking dish and cook in the oven for 10 minutes.

- Shake the pan to make sure they are not sticking. Add the onion, pepper and garlic and toss well. Add the olive oil only if the sausages have not produced enough fat to coat the vegetables. Season with salt and pepper. Return to the oven for 10 minutes until beginning to brown.

- Add the artichoke and tomatoes, stir well, then return to the oven for 10–15 minutes until all the vegetables are tender and browned.

- Serve with mashed sweet potatoes and some chutney, if liked.

Using the remaining artichoke hearts
- Use them in Paprika Seafood and Artichokes (page 50), or tossed with Vinaigrette Dressing (page 139) with a generous dash of chilli oil and plenty of black pepper.

Apple Sausages in Redcurrant Gravy

Another advantage of sausages is that you can cook just the number you need, so do remember to freeze them in twos or threes when you buy them. Farmers' markets are a great source of good sausages.

- Heat a pan and fry the sausages for about 10 minutes until beginning to brown.

- Add the shallots and fry gently for about 5 minutes until soft; there should be enough fat from the sausages but if not, add a little more.

- Mix the cornflour and wine to a paste, then whisk it into the pan with the wine and stock. Add the redcurrant jelly and rosemary. Simmer, stirring, for a few minutes until thickened.

- Continue to simmer gently for about 10 minutes until the sausages are cooked and the sauce is thick.

- Serve with mashed potatoes and peas.

Ingredients
2–3 good-quality sausages
    with apple
2 shallots, sliced
2 tsp cornflour
2 tbsp red wine
100ml chicken stock
2 tbsp redcurrant jelly
1 small sprig of fresh
    rosemary

To serve
Mashed potatoes
Peas

Crumble-topped Pork Mince

Ingredients
1 tsp olive oil
1 shallot, chopped
¼ tsp easy garlic
½ celery stick, chopped
1 small carrot, chopped
120g minced pork
Dash of white wine
120ml chicken or vegetable
   stock
1 tbsp tomato purée
1 tbsp chopped fresh parsley
Salt and freshly ground black
   pepper
3 tbsp breadcrumbs
3 tbsp rolled oats
25g cold butter, grated

To serve
Green vegetables or a salad

Pork mince makes a pleasant change from beef – lighter but still tasty and filling. If you prefer, you could make a larger quantity to freeze and serve in different ways.

- Heat the oil and fry the shallot, garlic, celery and carrot for 3 minutes until soft but not browned.

- Add the pork and stir until browned and separate.

- Add the wine and stir for 1 minute.

- Add the stock, tomato purée and parsley and season with salt and pepper. Bring to the boil, then simmer for about 15 minutes until the pork is cooked and the liquid has reduced. Spoon the pork into a shallow ovenproof dish.

- Heat the oven to 200°C/Gas 6.

- Rub the butter into the breadcrumbs and oats and sprinkle over the top. Brown in the oven for 5–10 minutes.

- Serve with green vegetables or a side salad.

If you make a larger quantity
- **Curried Pork with Potatoes:** Reheat the pork thoroughly in a pan with 1–2 tsp curry paste (or to taste), 200g can of chopped tomatoes and 1 peeled and diced cooked potato. Serve with rice or naan bread.

- **Chilli Pork with Tacos:** Reheat the pork thoroughly in a pan with 1 tsp chilli paste, 200g can chopped tomatoes and 1 tsp tomato purée. Taste and add more chilli if you like. Very thinly slice a shallot and shred a piece of cucumber and a few lettuce leaves and serve with tacos and guacamole or soured cream. If you don't have soured cream or guacamole, mix a dash of easy garlic into a spoonful of mayonnaise.

Pork with Grapefruit Sauce

The sharp tang of the grapefruit is softened by the maple syrup but still complements a rich meat like pork. It takes only minutes to prepare and cook, and is easy to adapt to suit your own taste.

- Peel the grapefruit and cut it into segments, cutting off all the pith and membranes.

- Melt the butter in a small frying pan, add the pork and fry for a few minutes over a high heat until browned, turning once.

- Add the wine, redcurrant jelly and 2 tbsp of the maple syrup and bring to a simmer, whisking until the jelly has dissolved. Season with salt and pepper. Simmer for about 5–10 minutes until the meat is cooked.

- Add the grapefruit and bring to the boil. Taste and season with salt and pepper, and some extra maple syrup, if liked. Simmer for a few minutes to reduce and thicken the sauce slightly.

- Serve with mashed potatoes and a steamed green vegetable.

Using the remaining grapefruit
- Enjoy it as it is for breakfast, or treat yourself to Grapefruit and Blueberry Brûlée (page 163).

Ingredients
½ grapefruit
1 tbsp butter
1 pork escalope or gammon
   steak
4 tbsp red wine
4 tbsp redcurrant jelly
2–4 tbsp maple syrup
Salt and freshly ground
   black pepper

To serve
Mashed potatoes
Green vegetable

Chicken and Poultry

The days of chicken as a special-occasion meat are long gone; now we eat more chicken than almost anything else, and it is available prepared in all sorts of ways that are ideal for singles, including breasts, legs, chunks and goujons. Although corn-fed, organic and free-range are often considerably more expensive, it is not only worth the extra for the flavour, but also for the animals' quality of life.

Turkey has also become readily available, and for our purposes, there's a particular interest in steaks, goujons and chunks.

Makes 1 serving

Chicken and Avocado Salad

Ingredients
Handful of rocket and/or
  baby spinach leaves
Chunk of cucumber, cut into
  semi-circles
3 mushrooms, thinly sliced
6 baby plum tomatoes
1 slice toast, cut into
  croûtons
1 cooked chicken breast,
  sliced
½ avocado, sliced
1 tsp lemon juice

For the dressing
1 tbsp honey
1 tsp balsamic vinegar
½ tsp Dijon mustard
Salt and freshly ground black
  pepper
3 tbsp olive oil

This is a delicious combination, put together in minutes and perfect for a summer evening served with a glass of chilled white wine. Do remember to treat your meals as an indulgence and really enjoy the opportunity.

- Arrange the rocket and/or spinach on a plate and add the cucumber, mushrooms, tomatoes and croûtons. Place the chicken on top.

- Toss the avocado slices in the lemon juice, then arrange them on the salad.

- Whisk together the honey, balsamic vinegar and mustard and season with salt and pepper. Gradually whisk in the olive oil.

- Drizzle over the salad and toss together to serve.

Using the remaining avocado
- Make into guacamole to serve with Chicken with Orange Salad (page 109), Crunchy Aubergine with Avocado Dip (page 124), or Spinach and Avocado Salad with Pancetta (page 36).

Chicken with Chorizo and Beans

You can use almost any kind of pulses for this dish instead of haricot beans, such as chickpeas, cannellini beans or red kidney beans. You can make it hot and spicy or milder, depending on your preference. Just adjust the quantity of chilli and paprika.

- Heat the oil in a pan and fry the shallots, pepper and chorizo for 5 minutes until the shallots are soft.

- Stir in the spices.

- Add the chicken and fry, stirring, until well coated in the spicy oil.

- Blend the wine and tomato purée and stir into the pan with the tomatoes. Bring to the boil, then part-cover and simmer for 20 minutes until the chicken is cooked and the sauce is rich and thick, adding a little water or stock if necessary. Season to taste with salt and pepper.

- Add the beans and cook for 5 minutes until heated through.

- Sprinkle with parsley and serve with rice.

Using the remaining beans, tomatoes and chorizo

- **Beans:** Use as a side dish with grilled meats. Try in Mixed Bean Salad with Chicken or use instead of butter beans in Butter Bean and Bacon Soup (page 28).

- **Chorizo:** Make Roast Potatoes with Chorizo (page 131), or slice into salads, or chop into Aubergine Boats (page 123) with the other ingredients.

Ingredients
1 tbsp oil
2 shallots, chopped
½ small red pepper, cut into chunks
1 chorizo sausage, thickly sliced
½ tsp smoked paprika
Pinch of chilli flakes (optional)
200g chicken goujons or chunks
2 tbsp red wine
1 tsp tomato purée
½ x 400g can of chopped tomatoes
Salt and freshly ground pepper
½ x 300g can of haricot beans, drained
1 tbsp chopped fresh parsley

To serve
Boiled rice

Makes 1 serving

Chicken Thighs with Spicy Dressing

Ingredients
½ tsp easy garlic
1 tbsp olive oil
1 tsp wine vinegar
½ tsp paprika
1 tsp Worcestershire sauce
½ tsp easy chilli
1 tsp honey
2–3 chicken thighs

To serve
Mixed salad
Crusty bread

You can make this with chicken wings if you like but I prefer chicken thighs or you could use portions. You can pile them on a plate of mixed salad with a sharp dressing, and serve with some garlic bread.

- Mix all the ingredients except the chicken and place in a bowl. Add the chicken and leave to marinate for at least 30 minutes, preferably overnight, turning occasionally.

- Heat the oven to 180°C/Gas 4.

- Grill or barbecue the chicken for about 20 minutes until cooked through, turning and basting frequently with the remaining marinade.

- Serve with a mixed salad and crusty bread.

• Chicken and Poultry

Chicken with Raisins and Pine Nuts

You won't use all the pine nuts in the packet for this dish but you can sprinkle them on salads or vegetables to use the remainder and they'll add a delicious flavour. You can toast the whole pack at once then cool and store them in the fridge.

- Heat the oil and fry the shallot, garlic and chicken for a few minutes until the chicken is lightly browned.

- Add the wine vinegar and herbs, then add the stock and raisins, season with pepper and bring to the boil. Simmer for about 15 minutes until the chicken is cooked through and the sauce has reduced.

- Toast the pine nuts in a dry pan, shaking the pan until the nuts are golden.

- Add half the pine nuts and continue to cook for a few minutes until the sauce is a thick glaze.

- Sprinkle with the remaining pine nuts and serve with rice.

Using the remaining pine nuts
- These appear in a number of recipes, including Minted Chicken Salad (page 114), Caramelised Red Onion Tart with Carrot Salad (page 128) and Lamb Cutlets with Sweet Spinach (page 81) but you can add them to any salad or sprinkle them on cooked vegetables or beans.

Ingredients
1 tbsp olive oil
1 shallot, sliced
½ tsp easy garlic
1 chicken breast, cut into
    strips
½ tbsp white wine vinegar
1 small sprig of rosemary
½ tsp chopped fresh thyme
150ml chicken stock
3 tbsp raisins
Freshly ground black
    pepper
3 tbsp pine nuts

To serve
Boiled rice with a touch of
    saffron

Makes 4 servings

Roast Lemon-infused Chicken

Ingredients
1 chicken
1 tbsp olive oil
Salt and freshly ground black
    pepper
1 lemon, quartered

For the stuffing (per person)
6 tbsp fresh breadcrumbs
1 shallot, finely chopped
1 tsp chopped fresh sage
1 small egg, lightly beaten

Buying a whole chicken is more economical than buying smaller joints, so it makes sense to apply the cook-it-and-freeze-it principle here. The stuffing quantity is designed for one, so if you are serving the dish for more, simply increase the quantities.

- Heat the oven to 200°C/Gas 6.

- Wash and dry the chicken, rub it with the oil and season with a little salt and pepper.

- Grate 1 tsp of the zest from the lemon, then put the lemon quarters inside the chicken cavity.

- Roast in the oven for about 1 hour, checking and basting the chicken occasionally.

- Meanwhile, mix the lemon rind, breadcrumbs, shallot and sage and season generously with salt and pepper. Add enough of the egg to bind the mixture and roll into 2 or 3 small balls. Add them to the roasting tin, roll in the juices and return the tin to the oven.

- Continue to roast for about 30 minutes, allowing about 40 minutes per kg. The chicken is ready when the juices run clear when you pierce the thickest part of the thigh.

- Remove from the oven, cover with foil, and leave to rest for a few minutes before carving.

- Cut off and serve one chicken breast.

Storing the extras
- Cut off and reserve the legs and the remaining breast. When cool, wrap, label and freeze the legs and the breast separately.

- Remove the remaining meat from the bones, pack into a freezer bag, label and freeze.

- Chicken and Poultry

- Put the carcase in a large saucepan, add an onion and a few carrots or vegetables and just cover with water. Bring to the boil, cover and simmer for about 45 minutes. Strain, discarding the carcase and vegetables, then boil to reduce by half. Cool, pour the stock into a freezer container, label and freeze.

Serving the remaining portions

- **Chicken with Pancetta:** Slice one chicken breast in half horizontally. Top each half with a slice of mozzarella and a sage or basil leaf, then wrap in a slice of pancetta secured with a cocktail stick. Fry in a little olive oil, adding a slug of white wine when almost done. Serve with a fresh mixed salad with a Balsamic Dressing (page 139).

- **Chicken Filo Parcels:** Defrost the stock and meat, and 6 filo pastry sheets, but keep it well wrapped as it dries out quickly. Blend 1 tsp cornflour with 250ml stock, add 2 tbsp redcurrant jelly and bring to the boil. Stir for a few minutes until thickened, then add the chicken and season with salt and a twist of black pepper. Brush the filo with oil and fold each sheet in half to make squares. Brush the edges with oil, spoon in some chicken, then twist the tops into little parcels. Brush with oil, then bake in the oven at 200°C/Gas 6 for about 10 minutes until crisp and golden. Serve with a cucumber salad.

- **Sweet and Sour Chicken:** Defrost the chicken legs. Blend 250ml chicken stock with 2 tbsp mustard, 2 tbsp brown sugar, 3 tbsp tomato purée and some salt and a twist of pepper. Bring to the boil, then simmer, whisking, for a few minutes until it begins to thicken. Add the chicken and cook for about 10 minutes until thoroughly heated through, and the sauce has reduced to a sticky glaze. Serve on its own or with egg noodles.

Makes 1 serving

Chicken in Lemon and Tarragon Sauce

Ingredients
1 tbsp plain flour
Salt and freshly ground black
    pepper
4 chicken thighs
1 tbsp olive oil
½ tsp easy garlic
Grated zest and juice of ½
    lemon
150ml chicken stock
1 tbsp chopped fresh
    tarragon

To serve
Wild rice
Sweet Tomato Salad (page
    130)

Tarragon is popular in classic French cookery but has gone somewhat out of favour. I'm not sure why because it works so well with chicken and fish in particular. You can use a breast or leg portion if you prefer.

- Season the flour with salt and pepper and toss the chicken pieces in the flour.

- Heat the oil and fry the chicken until browned.

- Stir in the easy garlic, the lemon zest and juice, stock and half the tarragon. Bring to a simmer, then simmer gently for about 15 minutes until the sauce has reduced and the chicken is cooked.

- Serve with wild rice and a tomato salad sprinkled with the remaining tarragon.

Using the remaining lemon
- Either seal the half lemon in clingfilm or grate the lemon zest and squeeze the juice and keep in an airtight jar in the fridge – there are so many recipes that benefit from a squeeze of lemon juice, it will not go to waste.

• Chicken and Poultry

Chicken with Orange Salad

This is inspired by the chilli offerings of the many city-centre outlets we enjoy. You could be surprised how easy it is to rustle up your own version. As always with chilli, adjust the quantity to suit your own taste.

- Mix the chilli, orange juice, honey, salt and pepper in a small bowl. Add the chicken and turn in the mixture. Cover and leave to marinate for at least an hour.

- Cook the chicken under a medium grill or in a griddle pan for about 15 minutes until cooked through, basting with any remaining marinade.

- Meanwhile, mix together the salad leaves, satsuma segments and pepper. Toss in the dressing and arrange on a serving plate.

- Arrange the chicken on top, garnish with the parsley and serve with rice.

Ingredients
1 tsp easy chilli
1 tbsp orange juice
1 tsp honey
Salt and freshly ground
   black pepper
1 chicken breast or
   2–3 thighs
Handful of mixed salad
   leaves
1 satsuma, segmented
½ yellow pepper, sliced
2 tsp chopped fresh parsley
A little Vinaigrette Dressing
   (page 139)

To serve
Boiled rice

Makes 1 serving

Barbecue-grilled Chicken

Ingredients
1 satsuma, juice and grated
   zest
½ tsp easy chilli
½ tsp smoked paprika
1 tsp Dijon mustard
1 tbsp honey
1 tbsp tomato ketchup
1 tsp olive oil
Salt and freshly ground black
   pepper
1 chicken portion

To serve
Mixed green salad
New potatoes

This is ideal for the barbecue but will work on the grill or even in a griddle pan. If you are cooking on a barbecue, make sure the chicken is far enough away from the hot coals to allow it the time it needs to cook through.

- Mix the satsuma zest and juice, chilli, paprika, mustard, honey, ketchup and a splash of olive oil. Season with salt and pepper and mix well. Add the chicken and leave to stand for 30 minutes, or longer if you have time, turning occasionally.

- Lift the chicken from the marinade and cook under a medium grill for about 15 minutes, turning and basting frequently until the chicken is tender and cooked right through and the outside is golden.

- While it is cooking, bring the marinade to the boil in a small pan, then boil to reduce by half.

- Serve the chicken with a fresh green salad and new potatoes, with the extra sauce spooned over the top.

Cook's tip
- If you don't have smoked paprika, ordinary paprika will be fine.

Makes 1 serving

Coconut Chicken with Sticky Rice

Thai curries are very popular and you can actually buy some excellent curry pastes, but it is fun to make your own using all the different spices. Many supermarkets sell packs of Thai spices in the fresh vegetables section.

- Grind the spring onions, ginger, garlic, lemongrass and chilli in a mortar and pestle.

- Rub the spice mixture all over the chicken.

- Heat the oil and fry the chicken for 7 minutes until browned.

- Pour over the coconut milk and bring to a simmer.

- Reduce the heat, cover and simmer gently for about 20 minutes until the chicken is cooked, stirring occasionally. Season with salt and pepper.

- Sprinkle with coriander and serve with boiled sticky rice.

Using the remaining coconut milk

- **Coconut Milk Shake:** Blend 250ml coconut milk, 2 scoops vanilla ice cream and 1 tbsp desiccated coconut and serve cold.

- Make Chicken Korma with Pilau Rice (page 117), add a spoonful to other curry dishes, or replace milk in cake recipes.

Ingredients
2–3 spring onions, chopped
1 tsp chopped root ginger
½ tsp easy garlic
1 small piece lemongrass
1 tsp chilli sauce
1 tbsp olive oil
2 boned chicken thighs
150ml coconut milk
Salt and freshly ground
 black pepper

To garnish
Chopped fresh coriander

Serve with
Sticky rice

Chicken Parcel

Ingredients

1 boned chicken breast
Salt and freshly ground black
  pepper
25g Gorgonzola or other
  cheese
2 slices of pancetta
1 tsp olive oil
3–4 baby leeks
2 tbsp dry white wine

To serve
Pasta

This takes a little longer to cook than some chicken recipes because the meat is tightly packed and thick, so do make sure you cook them thoroughly. You can use almost any cheese you like, so just see what you have in the fridge.

- Season the chicken with salt and pepper. Place the cheese on top, roll up and bind together with the pancetta.

- Heat the oil over a medium heat and brown the chicken on all sides for 10 minutes. Reduce the heat and continue to cook for about 10 minutes.

- Meanwhile, blanch the leeks in boiling water for 1 minute, then drain.

- Add to the chicken with the wine and continue to cook for a further 10 minutes until the chicken is cooked right through. As the chicken is rolled, it may take longer than usual.

- Serve with pasta.

Using the remaining pancetta and leeks
- Use for Leek and Gorgonzola Squares (page 127), Hake with Pancetta Potatoes (page 60), Spinach and Avocado Salad with Pancetta (page 36) or Chicken with Pancetta (page 107).

Crispy Spiced Chicken

Although this is not an Indian-style dish, naan bread seems to be just the right accompaniment. You could use pitta bread or any similar style of bread. Garnish with a wedge of lime or lemon if you have one.

- Mix together all the ingredients and leave to marinate for at least an hour.

- Heat the oven to 200°C/Gas 6.

- Arrange the chicken on a greased baking sheet and bake in the oven for about 15 minutes until cooked through.

- Serve with warm naan bread and salad.

Ingredients

1 chicken breast, cut into strips
4 tbsp plain yoghurt
1 tbsp lime or lemon juice
½ tsp ground cumin
½ tsp turmeric
½ tsp easy garlic
Salt and freshly ground black pepper

To serve
Naan bread
Mixed green salad

Minted Chicken Salad

Ingredients

1 chicken portion
150ml chicken stock
2 large handfuls of baby
  spinach leaves or
  watercress
1 tsp chopped fresh mint
1 tsp chopped fresh dill
2 tbsp Vinaigrette Dressing
  (page 139)
1 tbsp crème fraîche
2 tbsp toasted pine nuts

Poached chicken is useful as it remains moist and ideal for slicing for salads and lunch boxes. This salad has a fresh taste that is perfect for summer days. It's so quick and easy and offers a great combination of flavours.

- Put the chicken and stock in a small pan, bring to a simmer, then simmer gently for about 20 minutes until the chicken is cooked. Leave to cool in the liquid, then strain.

- Cut the chicken into strips and place in a bowl with the spinach and herbs. Drizzle over the dressing and toss together well.

- Serve with a dollop of crème fraîche on the top and sprinkled with pine nuts.

Using the remaining spinach and pine nuts

- **Spinach leaves:** These are great in salads, or simply wash and drain them, pop them in a saucepan with just the water clinging to the leaves and shake over a high heat until the spinach wilts. Serve with a grating of nutmeg over the top.

- **Pine nuts:** These appear in a number of recipes, including Lamb Cutlets with Sweet Spinach (page 81), but you can add them to any salad or sprinkle them on cooked vegetables or beans.

Chicken with Stilton Sauce

This is a very versatile recipe. You could use any blue cheese for this sauce: Dolceletta, for example, would give a milder flavour. If you don't have leeks, you could use a few spring onions for a similar sauce.

- Heat the oil and butter in a pan and fry the chicken in a griddle pan for about 5 minutes on each side until golden.

- Add the leeks and fry for 5 minutes until beginning to soften.

- Add the mushrooms and fry for 5 minutes.

- Stir in the Stilton and crème fraîche, making sure you do not allow the sauce to boil. Season with pepper and a little salt if necessary.

- Sprinkle with parsley and serve with a tomato salad.

Ingredients
1 tbsp olive oil
1 tbsp butter
1 chicken breast
2 leeks, sliced
6 mushrooms, sliced
60g Stilton, crumbled
2 tbsp crème fraîche
   (optional)
Salt and freshly ground
   black pepper
1 tsp chopped fresh parsley

To serve
Tomato salad

Chicken Korma with Pilau Rice

Ingredients

1 tbsp olive oil
1 shallot, diced
1 chicken breast, cut into
    strips or chunks, or turkey
    goujons
4 tbsp korma curry paste
½ tsp ground coriander
1 tbsp ground almonds
200ml coconut milk
½ banana, sliced

For the rice

1 tbsp olive oil
1 shallot, finely chopped
1 cardamom pod
2 cloves
1 small cinnamon stick
Pinch of saffron threads
1 bay leaf
100g basmati rice
150ml hot chicken or
    vegetable stock
Salt and freshly ground black
    pepper

It's a lot of effort to make a real curry so when I am cooking just for me, I cheat and use a good-quality curry paste. You can adjust the recipe to use a paste of your choice.

- Heat the oil and fry the shallot for 2 minutes.

- Add the chicken or turkey and fry for 4 minutes, stirring.

- Add the curry paste and coriander and stir together well. Stir in the ground almonds and coconut milk and bring to a simmer. Simmer gently for 20 minutes, stirring regularly, until the meat is cooked.

- Meanwhile to make the rice, heat the oil in a pan and fry the shallot and spices for 2 minutes.

- Add the rice and stir together to coat in the flavoured oil. Add the stock and bring to the boil. Season with salt and pepper. Cover and simmer for about 8 minutes until the liquid has been absorbed.

- Add the banana to the curry and heat through for a few minutes. Check and season with salt and pepper, then serve the curry with the rice.

Using the remaining coconut milk and banana

- **Coconut milk:** Use for Coconut Chicken with Sticky Rice (page 111) or make a Coconut Milk Shake (page 111), or add a spoonful to other curry dishes.

- **Banana:** Don't even try to pretend you didn't eat the rest while you were cooking!

Makes 1 serving

Turkey in Citrus Sauce

There are a lot of cuts of turkey in the supermarkets and it is very reasonably priced. Turkey goujons or escalope are ideal for one. If you buy a bigger pack, wrap and freeze the extras ready to use individually.

- Heat half the butter and the oil. Toss the meat in the flour, shaking off any excess, then fry for about 10 minutes on each side until cooked through and golden.

- Add the lemon and orange juice, and stock, and bring to the boil, stirring. Simmer for 5 minutes, whisking in the remaining butter if the sauce needs to be a little thicker. Sprinkle with parsley and season with salt and pepper.

- Serve with boiled rice and green beans.

Cook's tip
- If you are using a fresh lemon, add a little grated lemon zest.

Ingredients
1 tbsp butter
1 tbsp olive oil
1 turkey escalope
1 tsp plain flour
1 tbsp lemon juice
3 tbsp orange juice
3 tbsp chicken stock
1 tsp chopped fresh parsley
Salt and freshly ground
    black pepper

To serve
Boiled rice
Green beans

Turkey Goujons with Mushrooms

Ingredients

225g turkey goujons
1 tbsp plain flour
1 tbsp olive oil
2 shallots, chopped
½ tsp easy garlic
6–8 small button mushrooms
2 tsp tomato purée
250 ml chicken stock
Salt and freshly ground black
  pepper
1 tbsp crème fraîche
  (optional)

To serve
Green salad

There are plenty of ways to buy turkey now, which are ideal for the single cook, and goujons are particularly useful. You can cook the whole packet and freeze the extra portions, or divide them into smaller portions before you freeze them.

- Toss the turkey goujons in the flour to coat.

- Heat the oil in a large frying pan over a high heat, add the turkey add toss for a few minutes until browned.

- Add the shallots and garlic, turn down the heat to medium, and cook for about 3 minutes, stirring, until the shallots are soft but not browned.

- Stir in the mushrooms and cook for 3 minutes.

- Mix the tomato purée into the chicken stock and pour it gradually into the pan, stirring all the time, until the meat is bathed in sauce; you may not need all the stock.

- Season with salt and pepper and simmer, stirring occasionally, for about 15 minutes until the meat is tender and the sauce has thickened slightly.

- Remove from the heat and stir in the crème fraîche.

- Serve with a green salad.

Makes 1 serving

Sweet-glazed Duck

You can make this with legs or breast. If you use duck breast, cook for a shorter time so it is caramelised on the outside and still succulent and pink inside. Make sure you leave it to rest once cooked, then slice on the diagonal.

- Heat the oven to 200°C/Gas 6.

- Rub the duck skin with a little paprika, salt and pepper.

- Heat a pan and fry the duck for about 5 minutes on each side until the skin is brown and crisp.

- Transfer the meat to an ovenproof dish and place in the oven.

- Whisk the remaining ingredients into the pan, bring to the boil and boil for 2 minutes. Pour over the duck and return to the oven for about 30 minutes, basting occasionally, until the skin is shiny and caramelised and the meat is cooked through to your liking.

- Drain any excess fat from the dish, then leave to rest for 5 minutes.

- Serve with boiled potatoes and seasonal vegetables.

Ingredients
1 duck leg or breast
¼ tsp paprika
Salt and freshly ground
    black pepper
100ml chicken stock
2 tbsp honey
1 tbsp soy sauce
1 tbsp rice wine or sherry
1 tsp easy ginger
1 tsp tomato purée
½ tsp lime juice

To serve
Boiled potatoes
Green vegetable

Vegetables and Pulses

CHAPTER
11

We should all be eating plenty of vegetables and it shouldn't be difficult, as the variety and quality is amazing. As always, you will usually get the best flavours, not to mention the best value, if you buy in-season, preferably local produce.

Vegetarians should note that the recipes in this chapter are designed for anyone to enjoy so they do contain non-vegetarian ingredients. However, I have added notes to highlight how they can be adapted if necessary and, as always, you can add your own ideas.

For side vegetable dishes, an accompaniment of fresh steamed, boiled or otherwise simply prepared vegetables is usually the best choice. However, I have included a few dishes that can be served on the side or teamed with bread and salad for a main meal.

Artichokes and Courgettes with Balsamic Dressing

Ingredients
1 tbsp olive oil
2 shallots, sliced into rings
1 small courgette, sliced
½ x 400g can of artichoke
   hearts, drained and halved
3 baby plum tomatoes,
   halved
Salt and freshly ground black
   pepper

For the dressing
1 tbsp olive oil
Splash of balsamic vinegar
¼ tsp Dijon mustard
Pinch of sugar

This is a simple salad dish that's good as a snack or starter, a side dish or you can make it into a main meal by adding a chunk or two of ciabatta to dip into the dressing. If you don't have a griddle pan, a frying pan is fine.

- Brush the griddle pan with oil, add the shallots, courgette and artichokes and fry for about 8 minutes until browned both sides, with a clear set of stripes. Add the tomatoes for the last few minutes.

- Transfer the vegetables to a serving dish and season with salt and pepper.

- Whisk together the dressing ingredients and drizzle over the vegetables.

Using the remaining artichokes
- Use the remaining artichokes as a side dish, with dips, in Paprika Seafood and Artichokes (page 50) or Farm Sausages with Roasted Vegetables (page 96).

Aubergine Boats

Aubergines are rather like the Marmite of vegetables – you love them or you hate them. It's all about the texture. But as the flesh is mixed with lots of other ingredients in this recipe, give it a try even if you are not a big fan. You could be surprised.

- Heat the oven to 180°C/Gas 4.

- Slice the aubergine in half lengthways, brush with oil and season with salt and pepper. Place in a baking tin and bake in the oven for 8 minutes until beginning to soften.

- Mix all the vegetables with the tomato ketchup, sauce or passata and season with salt and pepper.

- Remove the aubergine from the oven, then scoop out and chop the flesh. Mix it with the other vegetables, then pile it back into the aubergine shells, putting any extra into the baking tin, or in a small ovenproof dish on the side.

- Return them to the oven for 10 minutes until cooked and beginning to brown on top.

- Garnish with coriander and serve as a starter or snack, or with crusty bread and salad as a complete meal.

Cook's tip
- This is a good recipe for the halogen as it only takes 10 minutes.

Ingredients
1 small aubergine
1 tbsp olive oil
Salt and freshly ground
    black pepper
3 mushrooms, sliced
2 baby plum tomatoes,
    halved
½ celery stick, sliced
½ red pepper, diced
2 tbsp tomato ketchup,
    Tomato Sauce (page
    136) or passata

To garnish
1 sprig of fresh coriander

To serve
Mixed salad
Crusty bread

Makes 1 serving

Crunchy Aubergine with Avocado Dip

Ingredients
3 tbsp olive oil
Dash of toasted sesame oil
1 tbsp soy sauce
Salt and freshly ground black
  pepper
1 small aubergine, quartered
  and sliced
1 tbsp plain flour
1 egg, lightly beaten
50g dried breadcrumbs
1 tbsp sesame seeds

For the avocado dip
½ avocado, stoned
½ tsp lemon juice
½ tsp paprika
½ tsp easy garlic
2 tsp chopped fresh
  coriander
2 tbsp olive oil

To serve
Rocket leaves

This is also good made with baby aubergines cut into quarters or chunks, depending on size. You can use the dip with crudités, too, or with any wraps or sandwiches.

- Mix 1 tbsp of the olive oil with the sesame oil and soy sauce, and season with salt and pepper. Add the aubergine slices and toss together quickly to coat.

- Dip the aubergines in flour, then in the egg, then in the breadcrumbs mixed with sesame seeds.

- Heat the remaining olive oil over a medium to high heat and fry the slices for about 8 minutes until crisp and golden.

- To make the dip, mash the avocado with the remaining dip ingredients and season to taste with salt and pepper.

- Serve the crisp aubergines with the dip and a few fresh rocket leaves.

Using the remaining avocado
- Use the avocado for Chicken and Avocado Salad (page 102) or Spinach and Avocado Salad with Pancetta (page 36).

For vegetarians
If you prefer not to use egg, you can dip the aubergines in water.

• Vegetables and Pulses

Coleslaw with Apple and Raisins

If you spot a small white cabbage, snap it up, as you can make this delicious coleslaw and use the rest as a vegetable with any grilled meats or casseroles. Or you can make it with Savoy cabbage instead.

Ingredients
½ baby white or Savoy cabbage, shredded
1 small eating apple, peeled, cored and grated
1 shallot, finely chopped
1 carrot, peeled and grated
Handful of raisins
4 tbsp mayonnaise
2 tbsp milk
Salt and freshly ground black pepper

- Mix the cabbage, apple, shallot, carrot and raisins.

- Blend the milk into the mayonnaise to thin it down, then season with salt and pepper.

- Toss the vegetables in the mayonnaise to serve.

Using the extra cabbage
- **Cabbage with Bacon:** Fry a chopped rasher of bacon and a diced shallot in a saucepan until just beginning to colour. Shred and rinse the cabbage, shaking off excess water. Add to the pan carefully as the fat will spit slightly, cover and shake the pan over a medium heat for a minute or two to soften the cabbage. Season with lots of black pepper and serve as a side dish.

For vegetarians
Use a vegetarian mayonaisse thinned with a little soya milk.

Chickpea and Aubergine Salad with Feta

Ingredients

1 baby aubergine, thinly
   sliced and quartered
1 tbsp olive oil
½ x 300g can of chickpeas,
   drained
2 tbsp flaked almonds
50g feta cheese, diced
Handful of rocket leaves
1 tbsp olive oil
1 tsp honey
½ tsp white wine vinegar
Salt and freshly ground black
   pepper

Try different combinations of ingredients, and make a note of recipe ideas in local restaurants when you eat out as chefs are always trying out new ideas. Keep an eye out for interesting ingredients in your local delicatessen or supermarket.

- Brush the aubergine quickly with the oil, then cook under a hot grill or in a griddle pan for 5 minutes.

- Mix the aubergine with the chickpeas, almonds and feta.

- Arrange the rocket on a serving plate and top with the remaining salad ingredients.

- Whisk together the oil, honey and wine vinegar and season with salt and pepper. Drizzle over the salad and toss together to serve.

Using the remaining chickpeas
- Use as a vegetable, add to a curry or a stir-fry, or purée with plenty of salt and pepper, a dash of paprika and enough olive oil to make a delicious dip.

For vegetarians
Use a vegetarian cheese.

Leek and Gorgonzola Squares

I always think ready-rolled pastry is a huge indulgence – but it's so easy! Use any flavoursome cheese you like – Gorgonzola is good, as is Stilton – but if you don't like blue cheeses, opt for a mature Cheddar, Gruyère or Emmental.

- Heat the oven to 200°C/Gas 6 and grease a baking sheet.

- Bring a pan of lightly salted water to the boil, add the leeks, then boil for 3 minutes. Drain well.

- Meanwhile, unroll the pastry on to the sheet and cut in half. Brush the edges with a little milk, then roll them up to create a case.

- Arrange the leeks in the case, then sprinkle with the cheese and spoon in the cream. Season with salt and pepper.

- Cook in the oven for 10 minutes until cooked and golden.

Serving the extra portion
- Serve the first tart hot, then slice the second for your lunch box the next day.

For vegetarians
Use a vegetarian cheese and cream.

Ingredients
100g baby leeks
Salt and freshly ground
    black pepper
320g sheet of puff pastry
A little milk
50g Gorgonzola cheese,
    grated
2 tbsp cream

To serve
Mixed green salad
Pickle

Makes 1 serving

Caramelised Red Onion Tart with Carrot Salad

Ingredients
1 tbsp butter
1 red onion, sliced
1 tbsp honey
1 tbsp balsamic vinegar
½ tsp dried thyme
Salt and freshly ground black
 pepper
75g puff pastry
A little plain flour

For the salad
1 carrot, grated
1 small orange, cut into
 chunks
1 tbsp pine nuts
Sprinkling of ground cumin
A little Vinaigrette Dressing
 (page 139) (optional)

You can make this in any size; small ones work well in the halogen. It does rely on the fact that you will have read the introduction and frozen your puff pastry in small portions.

- Heat the oven to 200°C/Gas 6 and grease and line a 15cm cake tin or two Yorkshire pudding tins.

- Heat the butter in a frying pan and fry the onion for 5 minutes until soft and beginning to brown.

- Add the honey and balsamic vinegar and fry for 2 minutes.

- Add the thyme, season with salt and pepper, and stir together well. Then remove from the heat.

- Roll out the pastry on a lightly floured surface to about 2cm larger than your tins. Spoon the onion mixture into the tins, not quite up to the edges. Place the pastry on top and tuck the edges down the sides to encase the filling.

- Bake in the oven for 30 minutes until golden and puffed up.

- Mix together all the salad ingredients. Dress with a little Vinaigrette Dressing if you like.

- Carefully invert the tart on to your plate, using the lining paper to help, and serve with the carrot and orange salad.

Ideas for Pasta

Pasta is perfect for one, and you can team whichever type of pasta you like with your chosen ingredients. I prefer a chunky pasta with a robust sauce and a finer pasta with a more subtle one.

Sauces for pasta

- **Tomato Sauce:** Use your own Tomato Sauce (page 136) or a ready-made and sprinkle with a few basil leaves and some freshly grated Parmesan cheese.

- **Cheese and Tomato Sauce:** Crush a garlic clove into a few spoonfuls of passata and top with crumbled Dolcelatte.

- **Pesto Sauce:** Pound 12 basil leaves, 1 garlic clove, 1 tbsp grated Parmesan, 1 tbsp pine nuts and 2 tbsp olive oil. Stir through hot pasta and top with Parmesan shavings.

- **Garlic Sauce:** Crush a garlic clove, whisk into a spoonful of extra virgin olive oil and season generously with salt and pepper.

- **Spinach Sauce:** Melt a knob of butter, then stir in a generous handful of fresh spinach leaves and a dash of milk. Cook until wilted, then season with salt, pepper and grated nutmeg.

Ingredients for pasta

- **Vegetables:** Lightly fried courgette slices; a few fried mushroom slices seasoned with oregano, salt and pepper; a sliced pepper.

- **Meat and fish:** Chunks of leftover cooked chicken or meat; crisply fried chunks of bacon or pancetta, cooked prawns, fish, canned tuna or salmon.

- **Pasta Carbonara:** Fry a chopped rasher of bacon with ½ tsp easy garlic until just browned. Whisk an egg yolk with 4 tbsp cream and season with pepper. Boil a handful of pasta until *al dente*, return it to the pan, stir in the bacon and egg and serve.

Ingredients

Quantity per person
2 handfuls of pasta,
   75–100g
Handful of spaghetti about
   2cm in diameter

Cooking pasta
Throw the pasta into
   boiling, salted water
Return to the boil
Cook for 5–10 minutes
   until *al dente* – to the
   bite
Drain and serve

Potato Pancakes

Ingredients
1 potato, peeled and grated
1 shallot, grated
1 bacon rasher, chopped
1 tsp chopped fresh parsley
Salt and freshly ground black
  pepper
1 tsp plain flour
1 egg, lightly beaten
1 tbsp olive oil

You can serve these on their own with pickles, add chopped cooked fish or meat, if you enjoy meat, or drained canned sweetcorn or a handful of frozen peas. Alternatively, make them a side dish with grilled fish or meat.

- Put the grated potato in a sieve and press out the excess moisture.

- Tip into a bowl and mix in the shallot, bacon and parsley, and season with salt and pepper. Stir in the flour and the egg.

- Heat the oil in a frying pan and fry spoonfuls of the mixture for about 4 minutes, pressing down lightly, until golden on the underside, then flip them over and brown the other side.

- Turn down the heat and continue to cook for 5–10 minutes until soft on the inside.

- Serve as a side dish or with salad and pickles.

For vegetarians
Omit the bacon and add some grated or diced vegetables.

Roast Potatoes with Chorizo

This makes a tasty dish to go with grilled meats, baked fish or even omelettes. It cooks well in the halogen oven, taking about 10 minutes on the top rack, although do be careful it doesn't burn before it cooks through.

- Heat the oven to 200°C/Gas 6.

- Cook the potato in boiling salted water for 3 minutes until just beginning to soften, then drain, shaking the colander to roughen the edges slightly.

- Mix the potato in a baking tin with the chorizo and garlic. Season with paprika, salt and pepper and drizzle with the olive oil.

- Cook in the oven for about 20 minutes, tossing occasionally, until the potatoes are soft on the inside and golden and crunchy on the outside.

- Serve sprinkled with parsley.

Using the remaining chorizo
- Use in Chicken with Chorizo and Beans (page 103), slice into salads, or add to the vegetables in Aubergine Boats (page 123).

For vegetarians
Substitute vegetarian sausages for the chorizo or use aubergine.

Ingredients
1 medium potato, cut into chunks
Salt and freshly ground black pepper
1–2 chorizo sausages, cut into chunks
1 garlic clove, chopped
Pinch of paprika
1½ tbsp olive oil
2 tsp chopped fresh parsley

Pesto Rice Salad

Ingredients
100g cooked long-grain rice

For the pesto
12 fresh basil leaves
1 garlic clove
1 tbsp grated Parmesan
1 tbsp pine nuts
1 tbsp olive oil
Salt and freshly ground black
  pepper

You can make your own pesto sauce or use ready-made, making this quick and easy to put together. Serve it with a mixed salad and cold meats, or with grilled meat such as lamb chops. It works both hot and cold.

- To make the pesto, pound the ingredients together, adding enough oil to make a loose paste.

- Blend through the rice and season well with salt and pepper.

Making a meal of it
You can add all kinds of ingredients to make this into an easy meal. If it's hot, try chunks of cooked chicken, prawns, fried peppers or aubergines. If you are serving it cold, add smoked salmon trimmings, diced ham or shavings of Parmesan cheese.

Makes 1 serving

Sweetcorn Pancakes

Serve these little pancakes on their own with some ketchup or pickle, with an egg or sausage for breakfast, or as a side dish with chicken. You can also make them with grated courgette, and make them larger if you prefer.

- Whisk together all the ingredients except the oil to create a thick batter.

- Heat the oil in a frying pan and fry spoonfuls of the batter for about 5 minutes on each side until golden.

Using the remaining sweetcorn
- Serve it as a vegetable with any meat or fish dishes, use for Chicken and Sweetcorn Chowder (page 27) or Pork Tortilla Wrap (page 90).

For vegetarians
Not suitable if you don't eat eggs.

Ingredients
½ x 200g can of
   sweetcorn, drained
3 tbsp plain flour
1 egg, lightly beaten
1–2 tsp snipped fresh
   chives, chopped
Salt and freshly ground
   black pepper
2 tbsp oil

Sweet and Sour Shallots

Ingredients

2 tbsp olive oil
250g shallots, peeled
3 tbsp sultanas
¼ tsp mustard seeds
Salt and freshly ground black
    pepper
¼ tsp freshly grated nutmeg
1 tbsp soft brown sugar
¼ tsp red wine vinegar
2 tbsp water

These keep in the fridge for a week or so and you can serve them hot with a grilled chop and steamed vegetables, cold with salad or cold meat, or chop them and mix them into hot mashed potato to serve with almost anything.

- Heat the oil in a small pan and gently fry the shallots, sultanas, mustard seeds, and a twist of pepper for about 5 minutes until soft.

- Stir the nutmeg, sugar, wine vinegar and water into the pan and season with a little salt and pepper. Bring to the boil, stirring over a medium heat until the shallots are tender and coated in a sticky glaze.

Creamed Sweet Potato with Honey

Apart from the superb flavour, the colour of sweet potatoes is such a great addition to any plate, and especially good to complement chicken or fish. They can be roasted, baked or boiled, but do try them this way too.

- Bring the potato to the boil in a pan of water, boil for about 8 minutes until tender, then drain and return to the pan.

- Mix in all the remaining ingredients except the chives and mash well, then beat to make a really smooth and creamy mixture.

- Stir in the chives to serve.

Ingredients

1 sweet potato, peeled and diced
2 tbsp butter
2 tbsp cream or milk
1 tsp honey
Salt and freshly ground black pepper
2 tsp snipped fresh chives

Tomato Sauce

Ingredients

2 tbsp olive oil
1 tbsp butter
2 onions, chopped
1 celery stick, chopped
1 carrot, chopped
1 red pepper, chopped
1 garlic clove
2 tbsp red wine
2 x 400g cans of tomatoes
6 fresh basil leaves
6 fresh parsley sprigs
Salt and freshly ground black
  pepper

A good tomato sauce is always useful to add to any number of dishes. Include a batch of sauce in a cook-in, then freeze it in suitable quantities to use when you are cooking; I think about 250ml portions is about right.

- Heat the oil and butter in a large pan. Add the onions, celery, carrot, pepper and garlic and fry gently for about 10 minutes until soft.

- Add the wine and cook for 2 minutes.

- Add the tomatoes, basil and parsley, and season with salt and pepper. Bring to a simmer, then continue to simmer for about 15 minutes, stirring occasionally, until the mixture is soft and well blended.

- Leave to cool slightly, then purée in a food processor. For a chunky sauce, leave it as it is; for a smooth sauce, rub it through a sieve. Check and adjust the seasoning to taste.

- You may want to simmer the sauce for 5–10 minutes to allow it to thicken. This will depend on your ingredients.

- Use straight away, or divide into 250ml portions, wrap, seal, label and freeze.

Using the remaining celery

- Use the rest of the celery in the base for other recipes, in salads (page 138), or for soup (page 32).

• Vegetables and Pulses

Stir-fry Vegetables with Chestnuts

You can buy vacuum-packed chestnuts ready to throw into all kinds of dishes. You can suit the ingredients for this stir-fry to what you have available – there are no hard-and-fast rules.

- Heat the oil and sesame oil and fry the shallot, carrot and pepper for 5 minutes until soft.

- Add the broccoli, sweetcorn, if using, and chestnuts and continue to fry for 3 minutes until everything is heated through.

- Mix the soy sauce and sugar, sprinkle into the pan and season with salt and pepper.

- Serve with noodles or wraps.

Using the remaining chestnuts and vegetables

- **Chestnuts:** These are sold in 200g packs. You can nibble them as they are; mix with Brussels or green vegetables; chop and add to meatballs; chop into stuffing mixes; add to a casserole.

- **Vegetables:** You should be eating plenty of vegetables, so you'll easily use the remaining sweetcorn and pepper.

Ingredients
1 tbsp olive oil
Dash of sesame oil
1 shallot, quartered
1 small carrot, sliced into batons
½ red pepper, sliced
3 broccoli florets
A few baby sweetcorn (optional)
4–6 chestnuts, halved
1 tbsp soy sauce
1 tsp brown sugar
Salt and freshly ground black pepper

To serve
Noodles or wraps

Ideas for Salads

*Throw away the rule book
when it comes to salads*
Mix fruit and vegetables
Include contrasting colours
Keep the main textures
crunchy
Add some soft-textured
contrast
Avoid one flavour
dominating the others
Keep it fresh

Salads are always best made with the freshest ingredients so buy in small quantities, use what you have, then try something else. That's better than wasting food or eating salad stuffs that are past their best.

- **Insalata Caprese:** This classic Italian salad is made by arranging sliced tomatoes and mozzarella on a plate, dotting with fresh basil leaves and drizzling with olive oil. A twist of black pepper is all you need to finish it off.

- **Mixed Bean Salad with Chicken:** A small can of mixed beans makes a filling salad; use a 300g can for a main-meal salad. Drain and rinse the beans, then stir in some chunks of chopped cooked chicken. Whisk a dash of chilli powder into a Vinaigrette Dressing (page 139), then fold it through the salad.

- **Fish and Beans:** Follow the ideas above but use cooked prawns or canned tuna or salmon instead of chicken.

- **Sweet Tomato Salad:** Layer a couple of sliced tomatoes with a spoonful of sugar, then pour over a little Vinaigrette Dressing (page 139), season with salt and pepper and leave to stand for an hour, if possible, before serving.

- **Watercress and Goats' Cheese with Honey Dressing:** Toss some watercress with cubes of goats' cheese and a few toasted croûtons (page 33). Warm 1 tbsp of honey, then whisk it into 2 tbsp of olive oil and drizzle over the salad.

- **Celery and Carrot:** Grate some carrot and mix with thinly sliced celery and a few sultanas or raisins. Dress with a vinaigrette sweetened with 1 tsp of dark brown sugar.

Salad Dressings

Match a robust dressing with a chunky, well-flavoured salad, and choose something more subtle for delicate flavours. Keep a dressing in the fridge for a week if you like.

- **Mayonnaise:** Beat 2 egg yolks with 1 tsp mustard and a pinch of salt. Very gradually pour in 300ml oil, whisking all the time, until the mixture thickens. Beat in a squeeze of lemon juice and 1 tbsp wine vinegar and season to taste with salt and pepper.

- **Aioli:** Make mayonnaise adding a crushed garlic clove to the egg.

- **Vinaigrette or French Dressing:** Mix 3 tbsp oil, 1 tbsp wine vinegar, 1 tsp Dijon mustard, a pinch of sugar, salt and pepper.

- **Balsamic:** Make vinaigrette with balsamic instead of wine vinegar.

- **Italian:** Add 1 small crushed garlic clove, 1 tsp dried oregano and 1 tbsp chopped fresh parsley to a vinaigrette dressing.

- **Thousand Island:** Mix 250ml mayonnaise, 80ml tomato ketchup, 3 tbsp chutney, 1 finely chopped spring onion and 1 finely chopped hard-boiled egg.

- **Ranch:** Mix 250ml mayonnaise, 4 tbsp buttermilk, 4 tbsp soured cream, salt and freshly ground black pepper, 1 finely chopped spring onion, 1 small finely chopped garlic clove, a pinch of dried thyme and 1 tbsp finely chopped fresh parsley.

- **Caesar:** Blend 250ml mayonnaise, 2 crumbled hard-boiled egg yolks, 2 crushed garlic cloves, 3 crushed anchovy fillets, 5 tbsp finely grated Parmesan cheese, 5 tbsp olive oil, 4 tbsp lemon juice, 1 tbsp water, salt and freshly ground black pepper.

- **Blue Cheese:** Mix 250ml mayonnaise, 250ml soured cream, 175g crumbled blue cheese, 1 tbsp wine vinegar, 1 small crushed garlic clove, salt and freshly ground black pepper.

Proportions
1 part vinegar
3 parts oil

Main oils for salads
Olive oil
Canola oil
Soya bean oil
Sunflower oil
Rapeseed oil

Add a little of
Sesame oil
Hazelnut oil

What to do
Shake the ingredients in a
  screw-topped jar

Eggs and Cheese

Quick and easy for singles, these ingredients are great for putting together a nutritious meal at the end of a busy day without too much fuss.

There are so many different cheeses available, there's a temptation – when out shopping – to buy more than you can eat, but do try to resist. Work your way through the cheese counter, trying a different one every week.

I usually use large eggs, so the recipes are written with that in mind. If you are using smaller eggs, you may need to add a little milk.

Makes about 8

Pancakes

Ingredients
1 egg
300ml milk
100g plain flour
Pinch of salt
Butter for frying

When my daughter went to university, she was amazed that people bought ready-made pancakes – and they were equally amazed that she made her own. They are great for sweet or savoury dishes, wraps or desserts.

- Beat the egg, stir in the milk, then whisk in the flour and salt until you have a smooth batter. Leave to stand, if possible, for 30 minutes before whisking again.

- Melt a small knob of butter in a small frying pan and heat over a medium heat. Swirl the pan as you spoon in a ladle full of batter so that it spreads thinly across the pan.

- Cook for about 1 minute until it moves when you shake the pan. Toss the pancake on to the other side and cook for 1 minute, then slide out of the pan.

- Add a little more butter and continue to fry the pancakes in the same way.

- Use as required or separate with sheets of baking parchment, wrap, label and freeze.

Extras, toppings and fillings
- **Herb:** Add some chopped fresh herbs, such as chives or dill, to your pancake batter.

- **Sweet:** Lemon and sugar; maple syrup; fruit compote; chocolate chips and ice cream; fruit coulis and crème fraîche; sliced banana and ice cream; brown sugar, sliced banana and pecans; honey and finely diced apple; blueberries and crème fraîche.

- **Savoury:** Ricotta cheese and chopped fresh sage; grilled courgettes and peppers; Mediterranean roast vegetables; shredded pork with a dash of harissa.

 • Eggs and Cheese

Potato and Onion Frittata

Since frittata and tortilla are both frequently called omelettes, I find the definitions highly inconsistent. This is a thick, baked egg and potato dish to serve in slices or chunks. It's ideal for the halogen.

- Heat the oven to 200°C/Gas 6.

- Bring the potatoes to the boil in a pan of water, boil for 2 minutes, then drain thoroughly.

- Meanwhile, heat half the oil in a frying pan and fry the shallots and garlic for 4 minutes until soft.

- Add the potatoes and fry for 5 minutes until browned.

- Spoon into a small greased ovenproof dish or cake tin. Pour over the beaten egg and cook in the oven for about 15 minutes until risen, set and golden.

- Turn out and serve with a tomato and watercress salad.

Ingredients
2 potatoes, peeled and diced
2 tbsp olive oil
2 shallots
1 tsp easy garlic
2 eggs, beaten

To serve
Tomato and watercress salad

Baked Eggs

Ingredients

2 rashers lean bacon,
    chopped
2 mushrooms, finely
    chopped
1 spring onion, chopped
2 eggs
Salt and freshly ground black
    pepper
1 tbsp cream or milk
1 tsp chopped fresh parsley

For the salad

1 tomato, sliced
Piece of cucumber, sliced
A few lettuce leaves

To serve

Toast or Melba toast
Mayonnaise (page 139)

This is a really old-fashioned dish but such a simple idea that it is a shame it has gone out of fashion. You can serve it with vegetables, but I prefer it with a crunchy salad. It works well in the halogen.

- Heat the oven to 180°C/Gas 4.

- Fry the bacon for about 3 minutes, then add the mushrooms and spring onion and fry for 5 minutes.

- Spoon into a greased ramekin or small ovenproof dish. Break the eggs on top, season with salt and pepper, spoon in the cream or milk and sprinkle with parsley.

- Bake in the oven for 10 minutes until the egg white is set.

- Arrange the salad on a plate with the toast and mayonnaise and serve the egg on the side.

Makes 1 serving

Leek and Gruyère Flan

Baby leeks have a delicate flavour and make a lovely tart. You can make it round if you like, but it looks great made in a square tin. If you don't have a square baking tin, use a cake tin.

- Heat the oven to 200°C/Gas 6 and put a baking sheet in the oven to heat. Grease an 18cm square tin.

- Roll out the pastry on a lightly floured surface and use to line the prepared tin. Prick with a fork and put in the fridge to chill.

- Boil the potatoes for about 8 minutes until tender, then drain and roughly chop into big chunks.

- Put the leeks in a pan of boiling, salted water and boil for 3 minutes, then drain.

- Whisk the eggs with the cream, chives, garlic and mustard. Stir in the Gruyère and season with salt and pepper.

- Arrange the leeks in the base of the pastry case and sprinkle with the potatoes. Pour in the egg mixture.

- Place the tin on the hot baking sheet in the oven and cook for 20 minutes until set and golden.

- Serve with salad and caramelised onion chutney.

Ingredients
120g puff pastry
1 tbsp plain flour
100g new potatoes
80g baby leeks, trimmed
2 eggs, lightly beaten
1 tbsp cream
2 tsp snipped fresh chives
½ tsp easy garlic
½ tsp Dijon mustard
30g Gruyère cheese, grated
Salt and freshly ground
   black pepper

To serve
Salad
Caramelised onion chutney

Cranberry and Brie Puffs

Ingredients
125g puff pastry
Flour, for rolling out
100ml cranberry and orange
    sauce
100g Brie, roughly diced
A little milk

To serve
Handful of rocket leaves
Caramelised Peppers with
    Couscous (page 41)

I have a little mould that cuts and seals pastry into a semi-circular pasty and I use that for these little puffs, or you can leave them open. Remember to split puff pastry into portions before you freeze it.

- Heat the oven to 200°C/Gas 6 and grease a baking sheet.

- Roll out the pastry on a lightly floured surface and cut into about six 7cm circles.

- Divide the cranberry sauce between the circles, spooning it on one half, then top with the cheese. Moisten the edges and seal together.

- Place on the baking sheet and brush with a little milk, then bake in the oven for about 15–20 minutes until puffy and golden.

- Serve warm or at room temperature as a snack, or with a salad of rocket leaves and accompanied by the couscous.

Cranberry and Orange Sauce

- If you buy ready-made cranberry sauce, simply mix in a squeeze of orange juice and 1 tsp grated orange rind.

- To make your own sauce, dissolve 75g sugar in 150ml water over a low heat, then stir in the juice and grated rind of 1 small orange and boil for 3 minutes. Add 225g cranberries and simmer for about 10 minutes until the berries burst.

Piperade

This is a classic dish, so easy to make, and is ideal if you really can't be bothered but still want something nutritious and tasty. You can serve it either hot or cold, so if this is too much for you, simply save a little for the next day's lunch.

- Heat the oil in a frying pan, add the onions and pepper and fry gently for about 4 minutes until soft but not browned, adding the garlic in the last minute.

- Add the eggs, stirring gently. Season with salt and pepper.

- Continue to stir over a gentle heat for about 3 minutes until the eggs are lightly scrambled. Make sure you do not overcook them – they are best still slightly moist.

- Serve at once with crusty bread.

Ingredients
1 tbsp olive oil
2 spring onions, finely
    chopped
1 small red pepper,
    chopped
½ tsp easy garlic
2 eggs, lightly beaten
Salt and freshly ground
    black pepper

To serve
Crusty roll

Omelette with Lots of Fillings

Ingredients
2 eggs
1 tbsp milk
Salt and freshly ground black
   pepper
1 tbsp butter or olive oil

For the filling
Choose from one or more of
   the following
Chopped ham
Grated Cheddar cheese
A few chopped, fried
   mushrooms
Smoked salmon trimmings
Canned crab meat, drained
Canned tuna, drained
Frozen chopped onions
A little chopped fresh
   parsley

To serve
Mixed salad

A well-made omelette stuffed with whatever you have in the fridge or cupboard makes a delightful meal served with salad or bread. Try some of the ideas below or make up your own. The quantity of filling is about a handful in each case.

- Lightly beat the eggs and milk in a bowl or jug. Season with salt and pepper.

- Heat the butter or oil in an omelette pan or a small, non-stick frying pan over a medium to high heat.

- Pour in the egg and swirl the pan so it spreads over the base of the pan.

- Turn the heat down to medium and gently cook the omelette for a few minutes, lifting the sides of the omelette to allow the unset mixture to run underneath.

- When the egg is set on the base, sprinkle the chosen filling over half the omelette then, using a slice, fold the omelette over in half, encasing the filling.

- Cook for just a minute or so until heated through.

- Serve with a mixed salad.

Savoury Egg Rice

You can use this as a side dish to accompany a curry, a Chinese dish or simply a grilled salmon steak or pork escalope, leaving out the fish or meat if you wish. Alternatively, add more vegetables and make it a more substantial meal.

- Heat the oil in a frying pan over a medium heat. Pour in the egg, stirring with a fork for a few minute until the egg is just beginning to set.

- Add the rice and keep stirring so the egg is distributed through the rice.

- Add the chopped meat, peas, parsley and five-spice powder, then season with salt and pepper.

- Continue to stir and heat for a few minutes until everything is piping hot and well mixed together. Serve at once.

Ingredients
2 tsp olive oil
1 egg, lightly beaten
½ cup cooked long-grain rice
2 tbsp chopped cooked chicken or ham
1 tbsp frozen peas
1 tsp chopped fresh parsley
Pinch of five-spice powder
Salt and freshly ground black pepper

Desserts

Many people don't serve a dessert when they are catering for one, or perhaps opt for some fruit or a yoghurt, which is a sound and healthy alternative with pretty much infinite variety. Occasionally, however, it is good to treat yourself and these tasty desserts are quick and easy to make and especially designed for one portion or for the freezer.

Fruit plays a large part in the selection because it is tasty, healthy and easy to buy in individual portions. If you fancy something more like a pudding, choose a portion of one of the cakes from the next section and serve it with a spoonful of cream, crème fraîche, yoghurt or ice cream.

Makes 1 serving

Chocolate Bread and Butter Pudding

Ideally, this is made the day before, but if you are just making yourself a little treat, you don't have to bother. It's easy to make a larger quantity, of course, if you have guests. Make it with brioche or brown bread for a change.

Ingredients
2 slices of bread
1 tsp butter
25g plain chocolate chunks
3 tbsp cream
3 tbsp sugar
1 small egg, lightly beaten
Pinch of mixed spice
150ml milk

- Spread the bread with the butter, then cut it into small squares or triangles. The books say you should cut off the crusts but I like them.

- Melt the chocolate, cream and sugar in a heatproof bowl set over a pan of gently simmering water.

- Arrange one-third of the bread slices in the bottom of a small ovenproof dish or pudding basin, spoon over one-third of the chocolate mixture, then make two more layers of bread and chocolate. Leave to cool a little, if you have time.

- Whisk the egg and spice into the milk, then pour it over the bread, cover and leave to stand for a couple of hours, if possible.

- Heat the oven to 180°C/Gas 4.

- Bring the pudding to room temperature, then cook in the oven for about 20 minutes until the top is crunchy but the centre still soft.

Halogen tip
- Another good one for the halogen, you'll need to cook it for about 15 minutes.

Caramelised Pears with Mascarpone

You can use whole nuts, chopped nuts or even chocolate chips to sprinkle on the pears if you like. Make sure you use a small, heavy pan and keep an eye on it all the time otherwise the caramel will burn and you will ruin the dish.

- Peel, halve and core the pear.

- Put the sugar and marsala in a small heavy-based pan and heat, stirring, for a few minutes until the sugar has dissolved, then stop stirring and boil the mixture for about 2 minutes.

- Add the pear and continue to boil for 3 minutes until the syrup turns to a golden colour, basting the pear occasionally.

- Beat the mascarpone with the vanilla until soft, then spoon on top of the pears and garnish with nuts to serve.

Using the remaining mascarpone
- Make Tiny Tiramisu (page 159) or serve it with other desserts. If you don't have mascarpone, or don't want to buy a whole pot, just use cream, crème fraîche or ice cream with the pears.

Ingredients
1 pear
1 tbsp caster sugar
1 tbsp marsala or a sweet
    sherry or liqueur
2 tbsp mascarpone
Few drops of vanilla extract
2 tbsp chopped mixed nuts

Makes 1 serving

Date Pudding with Toffee Sauce

Ingredients
3 stoned dates, chopped
4 tbsp water
1 tbsp butter
2 tbsp soft dark brown sugar
1 small egg
50g plain flour
½ tsp baking powder

For the sauce
50ml double cream
1½ tbsp brown sugar
1 tsp butter

To serve
Ice cream or crème fraîche

You can cook this simple little treat in the microwave for about 5 minutes if you have one, or it's perfect for the halogen, saving energy. If you have a second, smaller oven, get into the habit of using that.

- Bring the water and dates to a simmer in a small pan and simmer for 2 minutes until the water has been absorbed. Mix well to a purée.

- Heat the oven to 180°C/Gas 4 and grease and line a 600ml pudding basin.

- Beat the butter and sugar until soft, then beat in the egg yolk, flour and baking powder. Finally, fold in the dates.

- Spoon into the prepared tin and bake in the oven for about 30–40 minutes until firm. Turn out to cool on a wire rack.

- To make the toffee sauce, bring half the cream to the boil with the sugar and butter and simmer for 10 minutes until it turns golden.

- Remove from the heat immediately and leave to cool for 5 minutes, then whisk in the remaining cream.

- Cut the pudding in half horizontally and place one half on a serving plate. Spoon over half the sauce, top with the other half of the pudding and finish with the remaining sauce. Serve with ice cream or crème fraîche.

Chocolate Pudding with Built-in Sauce

This pudding creates its own layer of chocolate sauce as it cooks. It's deliciously gooey and a perfect comfort food as it's quite wicked! I use a 600ml pudding basin but any similar ovenproof dish will do.

- Heat the oven to 200°C/Gas 6 and grease a 600ml pudding basin.

- Cream together the butter and caster sugar until light and fluffy.

- Mix in the flour, cocoa, baking powder and egg to make a soft consistency. Spoon into the prepared dish.

- Dissolve the brown sugar in the boiling water, stir in the butter until melted, then pour over the pudding.

- Bake in the oven for 30 minutes until springy to the touch.

- Serve warm with cream or ice cream.

Halogen tip
- This is a good candidate for the halogen and cooks in about 20 minutes.

Ingredients
40g butter
40g caster sugar
25g plain flour
2 tsp cocoa powder
½ tsp baking powder
1 egg
50g soft brown sugar
50ml boiling water
Knob of butter

To serve
Cream or ice cream

Baked Apple with Caramel Sauce

Ingredients
1 tbsp butter
1 tbsp soft dark brown sugar
1 tbsp sultanas
1 tbsp dried cranberries
1 tbsp chopped mixed nuts
Pinch of ground cinnamon
1 large cooking or eating
   apple
A little lemon juice

For the sauce
2 tbsp butter
2 tbsp soft light brown sugar
2 tbsp treacle or golden
   syrup
2 tbsp double cream
Few drops of vanilla extract

To serve
Ice cream

My mum used to cook baked apples so this is an old-fashioned dessert that is best cooked when you have something else in the oven. You can use any kind of apples, although a Braeburn or a Cox are my favourites.

- Heat the oven to 200°C/Gas 6.

- Beat together the butter and sugar until soft, then beat in the dried fruit, nuts and cinnamon.

- Cut a line round the 'equator' of the apple and cut out the core. Squeeze a little lemon juice over the cut surfaces, then stand the apple in an ovenproof dish. Stuff the centres with the fruit and nuts and pile any extras around the apple.

- Place in the oven for 10 minutes, then reduce the oven temperature to 150°C/Gas 3 and cook for a further 20 minutes until soft and browned.

- Meanwhile, make the sauce. Melt the butter, sugar and treacle or syrup in a small pan, then simmer gently for 5 minutes, stirring occasionally.

- Remove from the heat and beat in the cream and vanilla.

- Pour over the apple and serve hot with ice cream.

Halogen tip
- This is another good one for the halogen, in which it will take 20–25 minutes.

• Desserts

Makes 1 serving

Rhubarb Oat Crumble

The almonds and oats make this a rather special crumble topping. I think rhubarb makes a particularly good crumble but you can use any fruit you like. Hard fruits, such as apple, would need to be pre-cooked.

- Heat the oven to 190°C/Gas 5.

- Put the rhubarb in an ovenproof dish and sprinkle with the sugar and water.

- Rub the butter into the flour and almonds until the mixture resembles breadcrumbs, then stir in the sugar and oats. Sprinkle over the fruit.

- Cook in the oven for 20 minutes until bubbling around the edges and crunchy on top.

- Serve with ice cream.

Halogen tip
- Cook the crumble for about 10 minutes.

Ingredients
4 sticks of rhubarb, sliced
2 tbsp sugar
2 tbsp water
2 tbsp butter
2 tbsp plain flour
1 tbsp ground almonds
1 tbsp soft dark brown
    sugar
1 tbsp rolled oats

To serve
Ice cream

Maple Syrup Tarts

Ingredients
50g butter
50g lard
200g plain flour
3 tbsp water
160g maple syrup
50g golden syrup
1 tbsp lemon juice
60g fine breadcrumbs
60g fine biscuit or cake
   crumbs

To serve
Cream or ice cream

This combines two of my favourite sweet things: treacle tart and maple syrup. You can make one large tart if you prefer, but making individual ones makes it easier to freeze and use them as you want them.

- Grease eight 9cm Yorkshire pudding tins or a 12 cupcake tin.

- Rub the butter and lard into the flour until the mixture resembles breadcrumbs, then add just enough of the water to bind the pastry together into a ball.

- Roll out on a lightly floured surface and use to line the prepared tins. Chill for 20 minutes.

- Heat the oven to 180°C/Gas 4.

- Warm the maple syrup and golden syrup in a pan, then stir in the lemon, and the crumbs. Spoon into the pastry cases.

- Cook in the oven for 15 minutes until golden brown on top.

- Serve with cream or ice cream.

- Wrap, label and freeze the extra tarts individually to use as required.

Halogen tip
- This works well in the halogen but my tins didn't fit so I used individual tin foil pie cases. They took about 10 minutes.

Tiny Tiramisu

This is a simplified version of the classic Italian dessert. It's easy to put together for one – this is quite a generous portion – or to make in a larger quantity. If you have a straight-sided glass dish, that presents the dessert particularly well.

- Beat the egg yolk until pale then beat into the mascarpone, followed by the sugar and espresso coffee. Fold in the chocolate chunks.

- Whisk the egg white until stiff, then fold into the mixture.

- Mix together the coffee and brandy. Dip half the biscuits in the liquid and arrange in the base of a small dish. Spoon in half the mascarpone mixture. Dip the remaining biscuits and arrange them on top, finishing with the mascarpone.

- Rub the cocoa powder through a fine sieve on top of the dessert.

- Chill until ready to serve, preferably the following day.

Using the remaining mascarpone
- Make Caramelised Pears with Mascarpone (page 153) or use a spoonful on other desserts.

Ingredients
1 egg, separated
5 tbsp mascarpone, beaten
1 tbsp caster sugar
1 tsp espresso coffee
50g chocolate chunks
2 tbsp coffee
1 tbsp brandy
6 boudoir biscuits, halved
1 tsp cocoa powder

Makes 2 servings

Chocolate Mousse

Ingredients
100g plain chocolate
1 egg, separated
2 tbsp caster sugar
150ml double cream

To serve
Cream or crème fraîche

Egg whites will not stiffen unless the utensils are grease-free, so whisk them first, then the other ingredients. This makes two rather generous portions but doesn't freeze so you'll have to enjoy it two days running.

- Shave a few curls off the chocolate and reserve for decoration.

- Melt the rest of the chocolate in a heatproof bowl set over a pan of simmering water. Leave to cool slightly.

- Whisk the egg white until stiff.

- Whisk the egg yolk and sugar until pale and fluffy, then carefully fold in the chocolate.

- Whip the cream until stiff, then fold into the mixture, followed by the egg white.

- Spoon into serving dishes or glasses and chill until firm.

- Decorate with the chocolate shavings and serve with a spoonful of cream or crème fraîche.

• Desserts

Makes 1 serving

Caramel Oranges

This is a simple dish that you can keep in the fridge for several days to make a refreshing end to any meal. It also makes a lovely dish to serve to guests as a dessert or to complement a sweet pudding and is easy to make in larger quantities.

Ingredients
100g sugar
100ml water
2 oranges

- Put the sugar and water in a small saucepan and stir over a low heat until the sugar has dissolved.

- Raise the heat and boil for 3–4 minutes until the syrup begins to turn golden.

- Meanwhile, cut all the rind and pith off the oranges, slice them across into circles, then halve or quarter to make bite-sized pieces.

- Place in a serving bowl and pour over the syrup. Leave to cool before serving.

Mango Sorbet

Ingredients

400g can of mango in juice
Water
250g caster sugar
Few drops of vanilla extract
Pinch of ground cinnamon
1 tbsp lemon juice

The great thing about sorbet is that you can leave it in the freezer and just scoop out whatever quantity you want. To make it even easier, you could freeze it in ramekins or ice-cube trays.

- Drain the juice from the mango into a measuring jug and top up with water to 250ml.

- Pour into a pan and add the sugar, vanilla and cinnamon. Bring to the boil, stirring until the sugar has dissolved, then boil for 1 minute. Leave to cool slightly.

- Purée the mango in a food processor, add the lemon juice, then pour in the syrup and process until well blended.

- Freeze in an ice-cream maker or pour into a freezer container and freeze, stirring to break up the crystals every few hours until frozen.

Cook's tip
- You can make a sorbet with almost any fruit purée.

Grapefruit and Blueberry Brûlée

Fresh grapefruit has that wonderfully sharp taste that creates a nice contrast with richer foods. If you have served a rich main course, this makes a great option for a refreshing dessert.

Ingredients
½ grapefruit
1 tbsp maple syrup
Handful of blueberries
Handful of grapes
2 tbsp crème fraîche
2 tbsp soft brown sugar

- Preheat the grill to high.

- Prepare the grapefruit by cutting round the outside of the segments, then cutting down the edge of each segment. Place it in a flameproof dish.

- Spoon over the maple syrup, then the blueberries and grapes. Pile the crème fraîche on top, then sprinkle generously with sugar.

- Flash under the hot grill for a minute or two to caramelise the sugar.

Using the remaining grapefruit
- Eat the other half for breakfast, or make Pork with Grapefruit Sauce (page 99).

Lemon Curd Ice Cream with Blueberries

Ingredients
300ml whipping cream
100ml Greek yoghurt
Grated zest and juice of 1 lemon
100g lemon curd
200g blueberries

You can make this when you have cream, yoghurt or lemons left over from other recipes, then it will keep in the freezer for you to enjoy a scoop or two now and then. Allow ice cream to stand at room temperature to soften before serving.

- Whip the cream until thick, then fold in the yoghurt, lemon zest and juice, and lemon curd.

- Spoon the mixture into a freezer container, cover and freeze for 5 hours.

- Serve with blueberries.

Cook's tip
- You can easily make just a small quantity by reducing the quantities in proportion.

Ideas for sweet sauces
- **Caramel Sauce:** Make a caramel sauce to pour over ice cream by melting half a Mars bar in the microwave or in a heatproof bowl set over a pan of simmering water. The other half will keep in the fridge.

- **Custard:** Custard from the chill cabinet or in cartons can be quickly warmed to pour over a slice of toasted panettone, or a toasted leftover brioche or warmed sliced croissant. Stir a spoonful of brandy or rum into the custard to make it extra special.

- **Chocolate Sauce:** To make the perfect chocolate sauce, melt 100g dark chocolate and 100g double cream in a heatproof bowl set over a pan of simmering water. Remove from the heat and stir in 100g butter.

Microwave Meringues

If you need to use up any small quantities of egg white, just mix in enough icing sugar to make a dough and microwave it. It makes a very crumbly meringue that keeps in an airtight tin.

Ingredients
1 egg white
300g icing sugar

To serve
Strawberries or other soft
  fruits
Fruit purée
Cream or ice cream

- Put the egg white in a bowl and sift in the icing sugar. Stir and blend until you have a pliable mixture.

- Roll it into small balls and place the first 3 on a plate lined with baking parchment.

- Microwave on High for 1 minute, watching as they puff up. If they sink immediately the oven stops, give them another 30 seconds. Remove and leave to cool.

- Repeat with the remaining meringue.

- Serve with fruit, fruit purée, cream or ice cream.

Cooking conventionally
- Whisk an egg white until stiff, then whisk in 70g caster sugar. Place spoonfuls on a baking sheet lined with baking parchment and place in the oven at the lowest setting for about 6 hours until they have dried out.

Cakes, Biscuits and Treats CHAPTER 14

Everyone needs a treat now and then, and since I really enjoy baking, perhaps my treats are more frequent than they should be! However, making a cake for one is completely pointless, so all these recipes are designed for your cook-in, so you make a normal-sized cake and freeze some of it to prevent you eating it all yourself!

Because it makes it easier to divide up, if necessary, and freeze, I often make square cakes or make cakes in loaf tins; they fit in the halogen and slot together much more easily in the freezer. Disposable metal trays are also a good idea. You can also make cakes in muffin tins and freeze them – then you can take out an individual cake. I have also bought some 13cm cake tins, which were sold as children's cake tins but make a great size for a cake for one or two.

Makes 1 serving

Cream Tea for One

Ingredients
2 tbsp butter
100g self-raising flour
1 tsp baking powder
1 tbsp caster sugar
1 egg
A little milk

To serve
Unsalted butter
1 small pot of clotted cream
Strawberry jam
Pot of tea

How you serve an individual cream tea is very important to enjoying it properly! Set the table with your cup and saucer, milk jug and pretty plates and indulge in a delightful tea and scones for one.

- Heat the oven to 200°C/Gas 6 and grease a small baking sheet.

- Rub the butter into the flour and baking powder, then stir in the sugar.

- Gradually add enough of the egg to mix to a soft dough. Roll out thickly on a lightly floured surface and cut into two large scones about 9cm in diameter. Place them on the baking sheet and brush with any remaining egg or a little milk.

- Cook in the oven for about 10 minutes until well risen and golden.

- Serve warm or cold with butter, jam and cream and accompanied by a pot of tea.

Cook's tip
- These cook well in the halogen.

Moist Chocolate Cake with Fresh Cream

This is my favourite chocolate cake recipe: simple and reliable. To serve now, make it in two 18cm or 20cm round cake tins. For freezing in portions, follow the recipe instructions using a rectangular tin, or use two 900g loaf tins.

- Heat the oven to 160°C/Gas 3 and grease and line 2 x 20cm square cake tins, or equivalent tins of your choice.

- Stir all the cake ingredients together with a wooden spoon or in a food processor until you have a smooth batter. It will be thinner than most cake mixtures.

- Divide between the prepared tins and bake in the oven for 35 minutes until the cakes spring back when lightly pressed.

- Turn out on to a wire rack to cool.

- To serve the whole cake, whip the cream until thick, then use it to sandwich together the two cakes.

- Sprinkle the icing sugar rubbed through a fine sieve or tea strainer over the top of the cake.

To serve some and freeze some
- Make the cakes and leave to cool but do not add the cream or icing sugar. Cut into suitable portions, then wrap, label and freeze. When ready to serve, defrost for a couple of hours at room temperature. Whip a little cream to sandwich the layers together, then sprinkle with icing sugar.

Ingredients
200g self-raising flour
2 tbsp cocoa
1 tsp baking powder
1 tsp bicarbonate of soda
175g caster sugar
2 tbsp golden syrup
2 eggs
150ml milk
150ml sunflower oil

For the filling
150ml double cream

To decorate
2 tsp icing sugar

Lemon Drizzle Cake

Ingredients
100g butter
175g caster sugar
175g plain flour
1 tsp baking powder
Grated rind and juice of
   1 lemon
2 eggs, lightly beaten
60ml milk
75ml icing sugar

Lemon is a wonderfully fresh flavour and here complements a lovely light cake. If you pop a lemon in the microwave for about 30 seconds before you juice it, you'll find you'll get more juice.

- Heat the oven to 180°C/Gas 4 and grease and line a 900g loaf tin.

- Cream the butter and caster sugar until light and fluffy.

- Stir the flour, baking powder and lemon rind together, then beat into the mixture a spoonful at a time alternately with the eggs.

- Add enough of the milk to make a soft mixture that drops off the spoon.

- Bake in the oven for about 40 minutes until springy to the touch.

- Blend together the icing sugar and lemon juice and spoon over the cake as soon as it comes out of the oven.

- Leave to cool in the tin, then remove and cut into slices to serve.

- Wrap, label and freeze the rest in individual portions.

Serving the remaining portions

- **Lemon and Frozen Yogurt Dessert:** Cut the cake into cubes and arrange half of them on the bottom of a dish. Spoon in some frozen yoghurt – lemon, raspberry or vanilla works well – then top with the remaining cake cubes and grate a little dark chocolate over the top.

- **Lemon Slices:** Slice the cake thinly and spread each slice with lemon curd. Stack the slices on top of each other, top with a mint leaf and a spoonful of cream to serve.

- **Lemon and Blueberry Layer:** Slice the cake, then arrange in the base of a dish. Add a few spoonfuls of crème fraîche, then sprinkle with blueberries and a little demerara sugar.

• Cakes, Biscuits and Treats

Toffee and Cherry Squares

This is an upside-down cake with a glistening fruit and nut topping when turned out. Line your tin and turn the cake out quickly, as indicated in the recipe, or it will stick. Try it with apricots, mango or other crystallised fruits.

- Heat the oven to 160°C/Gas 3 and grease and line a 25x30cm tin.

- To make the topping, sprinkle the almonds and cherries evenly over the base of the tin.

- Melt the butter and sugar together, then pour it over the fruit and nuts.

- To make the cake, cream together the butter and sugar, then add the flour, baking powder, ground almonds, eggs and almond extract and mix until well blended. Spoon evenly over the ingredients in the tin.

- Bake in the oven for 1 hour until well risen and golden.

- Place a sheet of baking parchment over the cake, then turn it over on to the paper on a wire rack, removing the tin. Use a large knife or palette knife to remove the lining parchment from what is now the top so you can push back any nuts or cherries that stick to it.

- Leave to cool a little, then cut into squares to serve.

- Wrap, label and freeze the rest in individual portions.

Ingredients

For the topping
150g flaked almonds
250g glacé cherries, halved
50g butter
50g soft brown sugar

For the cake
175g butter
175g caster sugar
100g plain flour
1 tsp baking powder
50g ground almonds
3 eggs
1 tsp almond extract

Honey-drenched Tunisian Almond Cake

Ingredients
175g butter
175g caster sugar
3 eggs, lightly beaten
1 tsp vanilla extract
6 tbsp honey
100g plain flour
2 tsp baking powder
50g ground almonds

I suppose I should say this is Tunisian-inspired rather than authentic, as it's my copy of a cake we loved when on holiday. For the best flavour, drizzle with a good-quality honey and enjoy the unique flavour.

- Heat the oven to 150°C/Gas 3 and grease and line a 900g loaf tin with a loaf tin liner.

- Beat the butter and sugar until soft, then gradually beat in the eggs, vanilla extract and 2 tbsp of the honey alternately with the flour, baking powder and ground almonds.

- Pour into the prepared tin and bake in the oven for about 1 hour until risen and golden.

- Remove from the oven but leave in the tin.

- Warm the remaining honey slightly. While the cake is still hot, prick the top with a skewer and spoon over the honey so that it soaks into the cake.

- Leave to cool completely, then cut into slices to serve.

- Wrap, label and freeze the rest in individual portions.

Old-fashioned Gingerbread

You can actually make this without ginger, as the treacle gives it that rich flavour and combines with the dark sugar and cinnamon to create a dense texture. It freezes well, too, so you can wrap and freeze in individual chunks.

- Heat the oven to 180°C/Gas 4 and grease and line a 25x30cm tin.

- Melt the butter, syrup, treacle and sugar.

- Add the flour, ginger, cinnamon and bicarbonate of soda.

- Add the eggs and hot water and mix to a quite runny batter.

- Pour into the prepared tin and bake in the oven for 40–45 minutes until well risen and springy to the touch.

- Turn on to a wire rack to cool and serve.

- Divide the rest into individual portions, wrap, label and freeze.

Ingredients
100g butter
175g golden syrup
175g black treacle
100g soft dark brown sugar
275g plain flour
1 tsp ground ginger
1 tsp ground cinnamon
1 tsp bicarbonate of soda
2 eggs, beaten
150ml hot water

Old English Beetroot Cake

Ingredients

200ml groundnut oil
200g soft light brown sugar
4 eggs, separated
3 tbsp milk
200g cooked beetroot, finely
    chopped
100g hazelnuts, toasted and
    chopped
170g plain flour
2 tsp baking powder
1 tsp ground cinnamon
¼ tsp ground ginger
½ tsp grated nutmeg

*For the icing for ¼ of the
cake*

30g icing sugar, sifted
80g cream cheese

We are used to carrot cake, so why not beetroot cake? It bakes to a subtle fuschia-hinted gold with a slightly dense texture. I have suggested you just ice a quarter of it and freeze the rest.

- Heat the oven to 180°C/Gas 4 and grease and line a 25x30cm tin.

- Put the oil and sugar in a food processor and process until well blended.

- Add the egg yolks and milk and mix.

- Add the beetroot, nuts, flour, baking powder and spices and mix until blended.

- Whisk the egg whites until stiff. Stir a spoonful into the beetroot mixture to lighten it, then fold the remainder into the mixture.

- Spoon into the cake tin and bake in the oven for about 35 minutes until a skewer inserted into the centre comes out clean.

- Leave to cool in the tin for a minute, then turn out to finish cooling on a wire rack.

- Keep one quarter. Wrap, label and freeze the remaining cake in individual portions.

- Make the topping for the first portion by blending the icing sugar into the cream cheese, then spreading over the top of the cake.

Using the remaining beetroot

- You'll get about seven beetroots in a 500g vacuum pack. It can be kept in the fridge for ages, but once opened, use it within a couple of days.

- **Beetroot and Brie Toasts:** Try the recipe on page 34.

- **Beetroot with Crème Fraîche:** Slice some of the beetroot and heat for a few minutes in the microwave, then serve as a vegetable with grilled meat or chicken, perhaps with a spoonful of crème fraîche and plenty of black pepper.

- **Marmalade and Orange Beet:** Dice a serving of cooked beetroot and place in a small pan with 1 tbsp butter, 1 tbsp finely chopped marmalade, and 2 tbsp orange juice. Heat, tossing occasionally, until most of the liquid has evaporated.

- **Beetroot Soup with Horseradish:** Mash or purée a portion of cooked beetroot with 1 tbsp lemon juice, 1 tbsp honey, a pinch of salt and plenty of freshly ground black pepper. Add enough water to make a soup consistency and serve hot or cold with a spoonful of horseradish sauce or soured cream.

Cuts into about 12 pieces

Chocolate and Nut Fudge Brownies

Ingredients
100g plain chocolate
100g butter
3 eggs
200g caster sugar
1 tsp vanilla extract
100g plain flour
100g chopped nuts
150g fudge chunks

This cake has the crisp top layer and gooey texture of brownies, with the addition of fudge chunks. You can buy packets of fudge chunks in the baking section, or just chop up fudge pieces so they melt into the mixture.

- Heat the oven to 160°C/Gas 3 and grease and line a 25x30cm baking tin.

- Melt the chocolate and butter in a bowl set over a pan of gently simmering water, stirring until smooth. Remove from the heat.

- Beat the eggs, sugar and vanilla for several minutes until pale and fluffy.

- Stir in the chocolate mixture, then the flour and nuts. Gently fold in the fudge pieces.

- Spoon the mixture into the prepared tin.

- Bake in the oven for about 30 minutes until a crust has formed on the top.

- Leave to cool in the tin, then cut into squares to serve.

- Wrap, label and freeze the rest in individual portions.

Coconut and Nut Squares

This is an American recipe, quick, easy to cut, freezes well and tastes good. Make your biscuit crumbs in the food processor, or put the biscuits in a paper bag and crush them with a rolling pin or milk bottle.

- Heat the oven to 180°C/Gas 4 and grease and line a 25x30cm tin.

- Melt the butter and stir in the biscuit crumbs. Press into the base of the prepared tin.

- Sprinkle the chocolate chips, coconut and nuts evenly over the base, then pour over the condensed milk and give the pan a shake to settle the ingredients.

- Bake in the oven for about 25 minutes until set.

- Leave in the tin for a few minutes, cut into squares while still warm, then lift out on the lining paper to a wire rack to cool and serve.

- Wrap, label and freeze the rest in individual portions.

Ingredients
100g butter
100g biscuit crumbs, about 6 biscuits
100g chocolate chips
100g desiccated coconut
150g chopped nuts
1 can of condensed milk

Banana and Date Bread

Ingredients
100g butter
225g soft light brown sugar
175g plain flour
1 tsp baking powder
1 tsp bicarbonate of soda
Pinch of salt
2 eggs, lightly beaten
125ml condensed milk
2 bananas, chopped
10 stoned dates

You can serve this as it is, or slice it and spread it with butter. You can even serve it toasted and spread with butter or lemon curd. It freezes well, in a cake or in slices, well wrapped, so you can take them out individually.

- Heat the oven to 170°C/Gas 3 and grease and line a 900g loaf tin.

- Put all the ingredients except the dates in a food processor and mix together. Add the dates and pulse once or twice so they are chopped into a few pieces and mixed through the cake.

- If you don't have a processor or mixer, beat the butter and sugar until pale and soft, then beat in all the remaining ingredients, squashing the bananas as you do. Chop the dates into three or four chunks and stir in.

- Pour into the prepared tin and bake in the oven for 1 hour until dark golden and springy to the touch.

- Leave to cool, then cut into slices to serve.

- Wrap, label and freeze the rest in individual portions.

Using the remaining condensed milk
- Try making Indulgent Chocolate Fudge (page 183).

• Cakes, Biscuits and Treats

Hazelnut Cake with Mocha Filling

This is a useful recipe for those who are gluten-intolerant – although don't reserve it just for them. Make sure you whisk egg whites in a clean, dry bowl otherwise they won't stiffen and treat the mixture carefully to keep it light and full of air.

- Heat the oven to 180°C/Gas 4 and grease and line two 18cm cake tins.

- Grind the hazelnuts finely.

- Whisk the egg yolks and sugar until pale and the mixture trails off the whisk in ribbons.

- Whisk the egg whites until stiff.

- Stir a spoonful of the egg whites into the egg and sugar mixture to lighten it, then gently fold the ground nuts and egg whites alternately into the mixture, keeping it as light as possible.

- Spoon into the prepared tins and bake in the oven for 30 minutes until springy to the touch.

- Leave to cool in the tins for a couple of minutes, then turn out on to a wire rack to finish cooling.

- Cream the butter with the icing sugar, chocolate and coffee until light, then use to sandwich together the cakes.

- Serve immediately, or divide into segments, wrap, label and freeze.

Ingredients
150g hazelnuts
4 eggs, separated
120g caster sugar

For the filling and topping
50g butter
50g icing sugar
1 tbsp drinking chocolate powder
1 tbsp instant coffee powder

Mocha and White Choc Chip Cookies

Ingredients
60g butter
60g soft dark brown sugar
1 egg, lightly beaten
Few drops of vanilla extract
80g plain flour
1 tbsp cocoa
1 tbsp instant coffee powder
  or granules
1 tsp baking powder
80g white chocolate chunks

On the border between a cookie and a cake, this makes a small quantity so you can give yourself a treat. Store them in an airtight container and they will last for a week. You can use different types of chocolate chip if you prefer.

- Heat the oven to 180°C/Gas 4 and grease a baking sheet.

- Cream together the butter and sugar until smooth and soft.

- Beat in the egg, vanilla, flour, cocoa, coffee and baking powder, then fold in the chocolate chunks.

- Drop dessertspoonfuls of the mixture on to the baking sheet about 2cm apart.

- Bake in the oven for 15–20 minutes.

- Leave to cool on the tray for a couple of minutes, then transfer to a wire rack to finish cooling.

Halogen tip
- This is ideal for the halogen as it's just a small quantity but do use the lower rack. They cook in about 15 minutes.

Crumbly Honey and Oat Bites

I've included a recipe to make just a few little sweet bites, great to finish a meal or take in your lunch box. You don't even bake them so they are ideal to make just a few.

- Put 6 cupcake cases in a cupcake tin.

- Melt the butter, sugar, honey and cinnamon.

- Stir in the cereal, sultanas or raisins, rolled oats and nuts and blend together. Spoon into the cupcake cases and press the mixture together.

- Chill until ready to eat.

Ingredients
80g butter
40g soft dark brown sugar
1 tbsp honey
Pinch of ground cinnamon
50g oat cereal or rice cereal
3 tbsp sultanas or raisins
30g rolled oats
30g chopped mixed nuts

Pineapple Upside-down Cake

Ingredients
75g butter
175g soft brown sugar
400g can of pineapple rings
  or chunks, drained and
  juice reserved
4 glacé cherries
2 eggs, lightly beaten
100g self-raising flour

To serve
Cream or custard

This is a real 'nursery' cake/pudding for me because we often used to enjoy it at home. You can serve it warm as a dessert, with cream, ice cream or crème fraîche, or cold as a cake – either way it's delicious.

- Heat the oven to 180°C/gas 4 and grease and line a 20cm cake tin.

- Beat 75g of the butter with 75g of the sugar until light and fluffy, then spread it over the base of the prepared tin.

- Dot with the drained pineapple.

- Blend the remaining eggs and sugar, then blend in the eggs alternately with the flour until everything is smooth and well mixed.

- Spoon into the prepared tin and bake in the oven for about 45 minutes until firm to the touch.

- Remove from the oven and leave to stand for a few minutes, then invert on to a wire rack to cool, carefully removing the baking parchment and scraping any topping back on to the cake.

- Serve with cream or custard.

Using the remaining portions
- Wrap, label and freeze the remaining portions to serve another time.

Indulgent Chocolate Fudge

This superb confection will really strain your resolve! When using chocolate, those with more than 70 per cent cocoa will give you the best flavour. Break the bar into pieces before you unwrap it.

- Line a 20cm square tin with baking parchment.

- Put the butter, chocolate and condensed milk into a saucepan and melt over a gentle heat, stirring occasionally. Do not let the mixture boil.

- Remove from the heat and stir in the vanilla extract.

- Stir with a wooden spoon for a couple of minutes until the mixture is thick and shiny.

- Pour into the prepared tin, then smooth the top with a knife dipped in boiling water.

- If you wish, sprinkle the top with the chocolate chips or nuts and gently press them down into the fudge.

- Leave to cool, then chill in the fridge before cutting into small squares.

- Store in the fridge.

Using the remaining condensed milk

- **Double the fudge:** Make double the quantity of fudge and vary the toppings.

- **Banana Bread:** Use it in Banana and Date Bread (page 178).

Ingredients
40g unsalted butter
250g good-quality plain chocolate
½ can of condensed milk
¼ tsp vanilla extract

Optional extras
10g plain, milk or white chocolate chunks, walnut halves, hazelnuts or almonds

Meal Planners

Use these meal planners to get you into the right frame of mind to think ahead about maximising enjoyment and variety and minimising work and waste. Then you can develop your own ideas.

Ring the changes with breakfasts of cereal, porridge, toast, croissants, scrambled egg or other favourites.

I've suggested a lunch dish every day but on some days, I expect you'll have a salad or sandwich.

I have included a dessert or cake on alternate days; on other days, have some fruit or yoghurt if you like.

Week 1

Day	Lunch	Dinner	Dessert	Storecupboard check for the week	Shopping list for the week		
Mon	Butter Bean and Bacon Soup (page 28)	Grilled Mackerel with Harissa Couscous (page 52)	Caramel Oranges (page 161)	**Dry goods** Couscous Long-grain rice Ground almonds Bicarbonate of soda Breadcrumbs Cornflour Plain flour Rolled oats Caster sugar Soft brown sugar	**Meat** Cooked chicken breast Boned chicken breast Lean bacon Pack of pancetta 1 shoulder of pork joint Sirloin steak	**Fruit** 100g black grapes 4 sticks of rhubarb 2 avocado 2 oranges Pack of baby plum tomatoes
Tues	Spinach and Avocado Salad with Pancetta (page 36)	Aubergine Boats (page 123)	Fruit or yoghurt			
Wed	Omelette (page 148)	Chicken and Avocado Salad (page 102)	Old-fashioned Gingerbread (page 173)	**Cans** Chopped tomatoes Butter beans Honey Golden syrup	**Fish** 2 mackerel fillets **Vegetables** 1 small aubergine Pack of beetroot A few carrots Head of celery Fresh coriander ½ cucumber Pack of baby leeks 1 red onion 2 red peppers Bag of old potatoes Bag of new potatoes Pack of mangetout 100g mushrooms Fresh parsley 1 parsnip 1 sweet potato 1 turnip Pack of salad leaves with rocket or baby spinach leaves	**Fridge and freezer** Natural yoghurt Brie Pack of Parmesan cheese Cream Gorgonzola Eggs
Thurs	Traditional Vegetable Soup (page 32)	Farm Sausages with Roasted Vegetables (page 96)	Fruit or yoghurt	**Jars and bottles** Lemon juice Dijon mustard Olive oil Balsamic vinegar Wine vinegar		
Fri	Beetroot and Brie Toasts (page 34)	Steak with Gorgonzola Mash (page 75)	Rhubarb Oat Crumble (page 157)			**Other** Chutney Crusty and granary bread 200g can of pease pudding Plain chocolate Black treacle Walnut halves
Sat	Rice and Beans (page 29)	Chicken Parcel (page 112)	Fruit or yoghurt	**Spices and condiments** Ground cinnamon Dried mixed herbs Easy garlic Ground ginger Ground mixed spice Paprika Passata Salt and freshly ground black pepper Stock cubes Wine		
Sun	Chilled Almond Soup (page 31)	Roast Pork with Gravy (page 92)	Chocolate Bread and Butter Pudding (page 152)	**Fresh** Butter Garlic Milk Onions		

Still in the freezer

Butter Bean and Bacon Soup x 3

Traditional Vegetable Soup x 3

Roast Pork x 3

Old-fashioned Gingerbread x 3

Day	Lunch	Dinner	Dessert	Storecupboard check for the week	Shopping list for the week	
Mon	Sweetcorn Pancakes (page 133)	Smoked Mackerel Risotto (page 61)	Fruit or yoghurt	**Dry goods** Baking powder Bicarbonate of soda Plain flour Pasta Spaghetti Risotto rice Rolled oats Caster sugar Soft dark brown sugar	**Meat** Pack of bacon 500g minced beef 1 chicken breast 600g neck of lamb **Fish** Pack of smoked mackerel **Vegetables** Pack of asparagus Pack of cooked beetroot 3 carrots Head of celery Fresh chives 2 leeks 300g mushrooms Fresh parsley 4 potatoes Bunch of spring onions Fresh thyme Tomatoes Bunch of watercress Coriander **Fruit** 2 bananas Fruit **Fridge and freezer** Small tub clotted cream Small tub crème fraîche Pack of goats' cheese Small tub natural yoghurt Pack of Stilton	**Other** Bread Breadcrumbs Can of condensed milk Packet of dates Jar of horseradish Jam Mint jelly Packet of chopped mixed nuts Oat cereal or rice cereal Jar of pesto sauce Packet of sultanas or raisins Can of sweetcorn Red wine Brandy
Tues	Asparagus with Poached Eggs and Parmesan (page 37)	Spaghetti and Meatballs with Tomato Sauce (page 67)	Crumbly Honey and Oat Bites (page 181)			
Wed	Beetroot Soup with Horseradish (page 175)	Arancini (page 62)	Fruit or yoghurt	**Cans** Borlotti beans		
Thurs	Cheese and Tomato Pasta (page 129)	Oriental Honeyed Pork (page 93)	Banana and Date Bread (page 178)	**Jars and bottles** Honey Olive oil Tomato purée Wine vinegar White wine Worcestershire sauce		
Fri	Brandied Bean and Bacon Soup (page 28)	Chicken Korma with Pilau Rice (page 117)	Fruit or yoghurt			
Sat	Pasta Carbonara (page 129)	Lamb with Minted Mash (page 78)	Cream Tea for One (page 168)	**Spices and condiments** Bay leaves Ground cinnamon Dijon mustard Dried oregano Salt and freshly ground black pepper Stock Worcestershire sauce		
Sun	Watercress and Goats' Cheese Salad (page 138)	Thick Vegetable and Bean Soup with Garlic Croûtons (page 28)	Fruit or yoghurt	**Fresh** Butter Eggs Garlic or easy garlic Milk Onion Parmesan cheese Shallots		

Still in the freezer

Butter Bean and Bacon Soup x 1

Traditional Vegetable Soup x 2

Meatballs x 3

Roast Pork x 2

Banana and Date Bread x 3

Old-fashioned Gingerbread x 3

Index

Almond Soup, Chilled 31
apple
    Apple Sausages in Redcurrant Gravy, 97
    Baked Apple with Caramel Sauce, 156
    Coleslaw with Apple and Raisins, 125
    Curried Apple Soup, 26
Arancini, 62
artichokes
    Artichokes and Courgettes with Balsamic
      Dressing, 122
    Paprika Seafood and Artichokes, 50
Asparagus with Poached Eggs and Parmesan,
    37
aubergine
    Aubergine Boats, 123
    Chickpea and Aubergine Salad with Feta,
      127
    Crunchy Aubergine and Avocado Dip, 124
    Stuffed Minted Aubergine, 80
avocado
    Chicken and Avocado Salad, 102
    Spinach and Avocado Salad with Pancetta,
      37

Bacon and Bean Cobbler, 29
Baked Apple with Caramel Sauce, 156
Baked Eggs, 144
Baked Stuffed Mushrooms, 70
Banana and Date Bread, 178
Barbecue-grilled Chicken, 110
beef
    Baked Stuffed Mushrooms, 70
    Beef, Bacon and Egg, 71
    Beef in Baked Potatoes, 73
    Beef Cobbler, 73
    Beef in Red Wine, 72
    Beef and Wine Pie, 73
    Cannelloni with Blue Cheese, 69

Filo Beef Parcels, 74
Home-made Burger with Caramelised
    Onions, 66
Minced Beef with Chilli and Kidney Beans,
    74
Minced Beef Pie, 69
Spaghetti and Meatballs with Tomato
    Sauce, 67
Spiced Beef Wraps, 74
Spicy Mince and Sweet Potato, 74
Steak with Gorgonzola Mash, 75
Steak Sandwich and Caramelised Peppers,
    41
Tagliatelle Bolognese, 68
beetroot
    Beetroot and Brie Toasts, 34
    Beetroot with Crème Fraiche, 175
    Beetroot with Lemon, 35
    Beetroot Soup, 35
    Beetroot Soup with Horseradish, 175
    Marmalade Beetroot, 35
    Marmalade and Orange Beet, 175
    Old English Beetroot Cake, 174
    Sliced Beetroot with Crème Fraiche and
      Pepper, 35
beginners, 20–22
Braised Tender Lamb, 84
Brandied Bean and Bacon Soup, 29
Butter Bean and Bacon Soup, 28

Cabbage with Bacon, 125
cakes
    Banana and Date Bread, 178
    Chocolate and Nut Fudge Brownies, 176
    Coconut and Nut Squares, 177
    Cream Tea for One, 168
    Crumbly Honey and Oat Bites, 181
    Hazelnut Cake with Mocha Filling, 179

Honey-drenched Tunisian Almond Cake, 172
Lemon Drizzle Cake, 170
Mocha and White Choc Chip Cookies, 180
Moist Chocolate Cake with Fresh Cream, 169
Old English Beetroot Cake, 174
Old-fashioned Gingerbread, 173
Pineapple Upside-down Cake, 182
Toffee and Cherry Squares, 171
Cannelloni with Blue Cheese, 69
Caramel Oranges, 161
Caramelised Onion and Goats' Cheese Puffs, 38
Caramelised Pears with Mascarpone, 153
Caramelised Pepper with Couscous, 41
Caramelised Red Onion Tart with Carrot Salad, 128
carrots
    Carrot and Coriander Soup, 30
    Carrot Soup with Mango Chutney, 30
    Carrot Soup with Tomato Bread, 30
    Hot Carrot Soup, 30
    Lamb with Carrot Mash, Celery and Carrot, 138
Celery Soup, 32
cheese
    Caramelised Onion and Goats' Cheese Puffs, 38
    Chicken with Stilton Sauce, 115
    Cranberry and Brie Puffs, 146
    Leek and Gorgonzola Squares, 127
    Leek and Gruyère Flan, 145
    Pork Rolls with Gorgonzola, 89
    Stilton Pâté, 40
chicken
    Barbecue-grilled Chicken, 110
    Chicken and Avocado Salad, 102
    Chicken with Chorizo and Beans, 103
    Chicken Filo Parcels, 107
    Chicken Korma with Pilau Rice, 116
    Chicken in Lemon and Tarragon Sauce, 108
    Chicken with Orange Salad, 109
    Chicken Parcel, 112

Chicken with Pancetta, 107
Chicken with Raisins and Pine Nuts, 105
Chicken with Stilton Sauce, 115
Chicken and Sweetcorn Chowder, 27
Chicken Thighs with Spicy Dressing, 104
Coconut Chicken with Sticky Rice, 111
Crispy Spiced Chicken, 113
Minted Chicken Salad, 114
Mixed Bean Salad with Chicken, 138
Roast Lemon-infused Chicken, 106
Sweet and Sour Chicken, 107
Chickpea and Aubergine Salad with Feta, 126
Chilled Almond Soup, 31
Chilli Pork with Tacos, 98
chocolate
    Chocolate Bread and Butter Pudding, 152
    Chocolate Mousse, 160
    Chocolate and Nut Fudge Brownies, 176
    Chocolate Pudding with Built-in Sauce, 155
    Indulgent Chocolate Fudge, 183
    Mocha and White Choc Chip Cookies, 180
    Moist Chocolate Cake with Fresh Cream, 139
coconut
    Coconut and Nut Squares, 177
    Coconut Chicken with Sticky Rice, 111
    Coconut Milk Shake, 111
Coleslaw with Apple and Raisins, 125
Cooking and Serving Fish, 46
Couscous, 52
Crab Balls with Dipping Sauces, 47
Cranberry and Brie Puffs, 146
Cream Tea for One, 168
Cream of Vegetable Soup, 32
Creamed Sweet Potato with Honey, 135
Crispy Spiced Chicken, 113
Crumble-topped Pork Mince, 98
Crumbly Honey and Oat Bites, 181
Crunchy Aubergine with Avocado Dip, 124
Curried Apple Soup, 26
Curried Pork with Potatoes, 98

Date Pudding with Toffee Sauce, 154
desserts
    Baked Apple with Caramel Sauce, 156
    Caramel Oranges, 161

Caramelised Pears with Mascarpone, 153
Chocolate Bread and Butter Pudding, 152
Chocolate Mousse, 160
Chocolate Pudding with Built-in Sauce, 155
Date Pudding with Toffee Sauce, 154
Grapefruit and Blueberry Brûlée, 162
Lemon and Blueberry Layer, 170
Lemon Curd Ice Cream with Blueberries, 164
Lemon and Frozen Yoghurt Dessert, 170
Lemon Slices, 170
Mango Sorbet, 162
Maple Syrup Tarts, 158
Microwave Meringues, 165
Rhubarb Oat Crumble, 157
Tiny Tiramisu, 159
Duck, Sweet-glazed, 119

eggs
Asparagus with Poached Eggs and Parmesan, 37
Baked Eggs, 144
Leek and Gruyère Flan, 145
Microwave Meringues, 165
Omelette with Lots of Fillings, 148
Pancakes, 142
Piperade, 147
Potato and Onion Fritatta, 143
Savoury Egg Rice, 149
equipment,15–16

Farm Sausages with Roasted Vegetables, 96
Filo Beef Parcels, 74
fish
Arancini, 62
cooking and serving fish, 46
Crab Balls with Dipping Sauce, 47
Fish and Beans, 138
Griddled Sole with Lemon Butter Sauce, 58
Grilled Mackerel with Harissa Couscous, 52
Hake with Pancetta Potatoes, 60
Paprika Seafood and Artichokes, 50
Poached Fish with Sweet Potato, 53
Prawns in Lime and Chilli Marinade, 48
Seafood Chive Pancakes, 51

Salmon Fish Balls with Chunky Sauté Chips, 56
Salmon with Herb and Garlic Mayonnaise, 54
Thai-style Salmon, 55
Niçoise Salad, 59
Salmon Fish Balls with Chunky Sauté Chips, 56
Sea Bream with Minted Salsa Verde, 57
Smoked Mackerel Risotto, 61
Smoked Mackerel and Potato Salad, 63
freezing, 13, 17

Garlic and Caramelised Pepper Bruschetta, 42
Garlic Sauce, 129
Grapefruit and Blueberry Brûlée, 163
Griddled Sole with Lemon Butter Sauce, 58
Grilled Mackerel with Harissa Couscous, 52

Hake with Pancetta Potatoes, 60
Hazelnut Cake with Mocha Filling, 179
Home-made Burger with Caramelised Onions, 66
Honey-drenched Tunisian Almond Cake, 172

Ideas for Light Meals, 42
Ideas for Pasta, 43, 129
Indulgent Chocolate Fudge, 183
Insalata Caprese, 138

lamb
Braised Tender Lamb, 84
Lamb Cheat Cassoulet, 79
Lamb Chops with Shallots and Peas, 82
Lamb Cobbler, 79
Lamb with Crisp Courgettes, 84
Lamb Cutlets with Sweet Spinach, 81
Lamb with Green Lentils, 79
Lamb with Minted Mash, 78
Lamb with Mediterranean Couscous, 84
Lamb with Parsnip Topping, 84
Lamb Steaks with Mustard and Redcurrant, 85
Lamb Chops with Shallots and Peas, 82

Lamb Shank with Rosemary and Garlic, 83
Stuffed Minted Aubergine, 80
leeks
Leek and Gorgonzola Squares, 127
Leek and Gruyère Flan, 145
lemon
Lemon and Blueberry Layer, 170
Lemon Curd Ice Cream with Blueberries, 164
Lemon Drizzle Cake, 170
Lemon and Frozen Yoghurt Dessert, 170
Lemon Slices, 170

Mango Sorbet, 162
Maple Syrup Tarts, 158
Mayonnaise, 139
Microwave Meringues, 165
Minced Beef with Chilli and Kidney Beans, 74
Minced Beef Pie, 69
Minced Pork Meatloaf, 95
Minted Chicken Salad, 114
Mixed Bean Salad with Chicken, 138
Mocha and White Choc Chip Cookies, 180
Moist Chocolate Cake with Fresh Cream, 169

Niçoise Salad, 59

Old English Beetroot Cake, 174
Old-fashioned Gingerbread, 173
Omelette with Lots of Fillings,148
pancakes
Pancakes, 142
Seafood Chive Pancakes, 51
Sweetcorn Pancakes, 133
Pan-fried Scallops with Prawns, 49
Paprika Seafood and Artichokes, 50
pasta
Cannelloni with Blue Cheese, 69
Cheese and Herb Pasta, 43
Ideas for Pasta, 43, 129
Pasta with Caramelised Peppers and Cheese, 41
Pasta Carbonara, 129
Pesto and Parmesan Pasta, 43
Pork with Lemon Pasta, 88

Spaghetti and Meatballs with Tomato Sauce, 67
Tagliatelle Bolognese, 68
Tomato and Chilli Pasta, 43
Pesto Rice Salad, 132
Pesto and Pasta Parmesan, 43
Pesto Sauce 129
Pineapple Upside-down Cake, 182
Piperade, 147
Poached Fish with Sweet Potato, 53
pork
Apple Sausages in Redcurrant Gravy, 97
Chilli Pork with Tacos, 98
Crumble-topped Pork Mince, 98
Farm Sausages with Roasted Vegetables, 96
Oriental Honeyed Pork, 93
Minced Pork Meatloaf, 95
Pork Escalope with Rhubarb, 91
Pork Fries, 93
Pork with Grapefruit Sauce, 99
Pork with Lemon Pasta, 88
Pork Rolls with Gorgonzola, 89
Pork Tortilla Wraps, 90
Pork Wraps, 93
Roast Pork with Gravy, 92
Soy Pork Noodles, 94
potatoes
Lamb with Minted Mash, 78
Potato and Onion Fritatta, 143
Potato Pancakes, 130
Roast Potatoes with Chorizo, 131
Steak with Gorgonzola Mash, 75
prawns
Prawns in Lime and Chilli Marinade, 48
Pan-fried Scallops with Prawns, 49
Quick Oriental Prawn Noodles, 39

Quick Oriental Prawn Noodles, 39

Rhubarb Oat Crumble, 157
Roast Lemon-infused Chicken, 106
Roast Pork with Gravy, 92
Roast Potatoes with Chorizo, 131

salads
Caramelised Red Onion Tart with Carrot Salad, 128
Celery and Carrot, 138
Chickpea and Aubergine Salad with Feta, 126
Coleslaw with Apple and Raisins, 125
Fish and Beans, 138
Ideas for Salads, 138
Insalata Caprese, 138
Minted Chicken Salad, 114
Mixed Bean Salad with Chicken, 138
Niçoise Salad, 59
Spinach and Avocado Salad with Pancetta, 36
Sweet Tomato Salad, 138
Watercress and Goats' Cheese with Honey Dressing, 138
Salad Dressings, 139
salmon
Salmon Fish Balls with Chunky Sauté Chips, 56
Salmon with Herb and Garlic Mayonnaise, 54
Thai-style Salmon, 55
sauces
Cheese and Tomato Sauce, 129
Pesto Sauce, 129
Spinach Sauce, 129
Tomato Sauce, 136
White Sauce, 69
Savoury Egg Rice, 149
Sea Bream with Minted Salsa Verde, 57
Seafood Chive Pancakes, 51
Shallots, Sweet and Sour, 134
Smoked Mackerel and Potato Salad, 63
Smoked Mackerel Risotto, 61
Sole with Lemon Butter Sauce, Griddled, 58
Soy Pork Noodles, 94
Spaghetti and Meatballs with Tomato Sauce, 67
Spiced Beef Wraps, 74
Spicy Mince with Sweet Potato, 74

Spinach and Avocado Salad with Pancetta, 36
Spinach Sauce, 129
Steak with Gorgonzola Mash, 75
Steak Sandwich with Caramelised Peppers, 41
Stilton Pâté, 40
Stir-fry Vegetables with Chestnuts, 137
Stuffed Minted Aubergine, 80
Sweet and Sour Chicken, 107
Sweet and Sour Shallots, 134
Sweet Tomato Salad, 138
Sweetcorn Pancakes, 133
Sweet-glazed Duck, 119

Tagliatelle Bolognese, 68
Thai-style Salmon, 55
Thick Vegetable and Bean Soup with Garlic Croutons, 32
Tiny Tiramisu, 159
Toffee and Cherry Squares, 171
Tomato Sauce, 136
Tomato and Chilli Pasta, 43
Traditional Vegetable Soup, 32
turkey
Turkey in Citrus Sauce, 117
Turkey Goujons with Mushrooms, 118

vegetables
Artichokes and Courgettes with Balsamic Dressing, 122
Aubergine Boats, 123
Cream of Vegetable Soup, 32
Crunchy Aubergine with Avocado Dip, 124
Coleslaw with Apple and Raisins, 125
Old English Beetroot Cake, 174
Stir-fry Vegetables with Chestnuts, 137
Traditional Vegetable Soup, 32
Thick Vegetable and Bean Soup with Garlic Croutons, 32
Vegetable Soup with Pasta and Pesto, 32

Watercress and Goats' Cheese with Honey Dressing, 138